SENSATIONAL
PRESERVES

SENSATIONAL
PRESERVES

HILAIRE WALDEN

Photography by David Gill

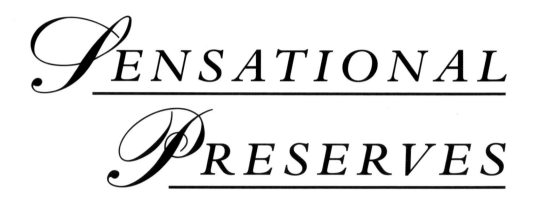

CONRAN OCTOPUS

First published in 1995 by
Conran Octopus Limited
37 Shelton Street
London WC2H 9HN

Reprinted 1996

A catalogue record of this book is available from the British Library.
ISBN 1-85029-708-8

COMMISSIONING EDITOR: Sarah Pearce
PROJECT EDITOR: Charlotte Coleman-Smith
ART EDITOR: Sue Storey
COPY EDITOR: Beverly Le Blanc
HOME ECONOMIST: Meg Jansz
PHOTOGRAPHIC STYLIST: Hilary Guy
PRODUCTION: Mano Mylvaganam
INDEX: Hilary Bird

Printed in Hong Kong
Produced by Mandarin Offset Limited

CONTENTS

$\mathscr{F}$OREWORD

Preserves add enormous variety to cooking and eating and provide an endless fund of ideas, whether you want to make a quick snack, add a new twist to a main meal or perhaps create an unusual filling for a cake or pudding. They can be used as accompaniments for both sweet and savoury dishes, in sauces, salad dressings and drinks, and even in casseroles and sorbets.

Preserves solve many a present problem. A prettily decked-out bottle or jar of a home-made preserve is always well received and is one of the most cost-efficient ways of making your own gifts.

Although there is a wide and cosmopolitan range of commercial products available, it does not match the eclectic selection you can make in your own home. The feeling of satisfaction from having prepared a batch of crimson strawberry conserve or glowing amber jam to put by for the autumn, cannot be denied. Neither can the gratification of seeing a neat row of your own home-made preserves lined up in your store cupboard.

Above: this superb Fig Conserve (see page 93) is one of the many exotic preserves that are easily made at home.

You will find that making preserves is not difficult; many recipes can be made by very inexperienced cooks. The equipment is very simple and you will probably already have all that is needed in your own kitchen. If you do not have access to home-grown fruit and vegetables, it is a good idea to make use of one of the increasing number of pick-your-own outlets. There is no need to make preserves in vast quantities so I have deliberately kept amounts down to practical and relevant levels.

In this book you will find recipes for preserves from around the world. You can also have fun blending spices and combining fruits and vegetables to make your own unique permutations, whether you want an unusual flavour or something less exotic.

ESSENTIAL INGREDIENTS

PECTIN is a natural gum-like substance found in the cells of fruit. Pectin is extracted from fruit by acid (also present in the fruit) during cooking and, when cooked with sugar, it produces a set. Under-ripe fruit contains more pectin than ripe fruit.

Pectin Content of Fruits

High	Medium	Low
Blackcurrants	Eating apples	Bananas
Cooking apples	Apricots	Blueberries
Crab apples	Bilberries	Cherries
Cranberries	Blackberries	Elderberries
Damsons	Cranberries	Figs
Gooseberries	Greengages	Grapes
Lemons	Loganberries	Guavas
Limes	Mulberries	Japonicas
Medlars	Plums	Mangoes
Oranges,	Raspberries	Melons
esp. Seville		Nectarines
Plums		Peaches
(some varieties)		Pineapple
Quinces		Rhubarb
Redcurrants		Strawberries

Fruits that are very low in pectin are usually combined with a high-pectin fruit or with lemon juice. Commercial sugar with pectin or liquid pectin can also be used, or you can make your own home-made pectin extract (see below).

Testing for Pectin: chop 900g/2lb apple peelings and cores (or whole sour cooking apples, windfalls or crab apples), cover with 570-900ml/1-1⅔ pints water and simmer gently, stirring occasionally, for about 45 minutes until pulpy. Tip the contents of the pan into a scalded jelly bag suspended over a large bowl (see page 17) and leave to strain, undisturbed, in a cool place for 8-12 hours. Put 1 teaspoon of the strained juice in a jar and add 1 tablespoon methylated spirits. Cover the jar and shake it, then leave to stand for 5 minutes. If a jelly-like clot forms (pectin extract), then the juice has a good pectin content. This test can also be used to test the pectin content of fruit after it has had its first cooking. Store the pectin extract in the refrigerator once you have made it. Use 150-300ml/5-10fl oz of the extract for every 1.8kg/4lb low-pectin fruit and add it to the fruit after it has been cooked, but before the sugar is added.

ACID is either naturally present in fruit or can be added in the form of citric acid or lemon juice. It is essential for a good set. The acid level in fruits declines as they ripen, which is why slightly under-ripe fruits are often recommended. Wild or late-season cultivated blackberries, as well as strawberries, pears, eating apples, cherries and vegetables such as marrows all need additional acid. Allow ½ teaspoon citric acid or 2 tablespoons lemon juice to 1.8kg/4lb low-pectin fruit.

SUGAR is needed for preservation, for flavour and for setting jams, jellies, marmalades and conserves (these preserves must contain sufficient sugar, pectin and acid in order to set). The more pectin a fruit contains, the more sugar it will set. If fruit has a high pectin content, 675g/1½lb sugar can be added to 450g/1lb fruit. Fruit with a medium pectin content will need an equal weight of sugar. If fruit has a low pectin content, acid and pectin must be added as well as an equal quantity of sugar to fruit.

It is important to use the right amount of sugar to make sure a preserve will set. Too little sugar will result in fermentation; too much will hinder setting and may cause crystallization.

If sugar is added to a preserve before the fruit is really soft, the fruit will harden and no amount of cooking will tenderize it. This hardening effect can be used deliberately. If, for example, you want very soft fruit such as strawberries and raspberries to remain whole, sprinkle them with sugar and leave overnight before cooking.

Granulated sugar is most widely used for sweet preserves, but lump and preserving sugars are useful as they form less scum and produce slightly brighter, clearer results. *Commercial sugar with pectin* contains apple pectin and tartaric acid; it is therefore very useful when making preserves from low-pectin fruits. The time needed to boil the preserve to reach setting point after adding the sugar is reduced to about 4 minutes. *Brown sugar* can be used for sweet preserves but it takes longer to dissolve and affects the colour and flavour of the preserve. It is more often used for savoury preserves.

Honey has a distinctive flavour and should only be substituted for a small proportion of the sugar. Honey can hinder the ability of a preserve to reach setting point.

Warming sugar: sugar will dissolve more quickly if it is warm. Put the required amount of sugar in a heatproof bowl, then place in an oven, preheated to its lowest setting, for about 20 minutes or until the sugar is warm but not hot.

SALT table salt is not suitable (except for brining pickles) as it contains additives to keep it free-flowing; these can cause discoloration and may inhibit some preservative qualities. Instead use pure rock salt or sea salt.

VINEGAR I use red or white wine vinegars because they have a more subtle flavour than harsh malt vinegar, which, strictly speaking, is not a true vinegar. Cider vinegar is used for fruity chutneys and relishes.

TYPES OF PRESERVE

JAM a thick, sweet preserve containing pieces of fruit or fruits. It should hold its shape without being too runny or too solid.
WATCHPOINTS see *Making Jams* (pages 14-15)
Sugar-reduced jam the quantity of sugar should not be reduced by more than 20% or the jam will be runny and will not keep for more than 3-4 weeks in a cool place, or 6 weeks in a refrigerator.
Freezer jam this is quick to make and has a fresh taste and a softer set than conventional jams. The fruit is not cooked in this type of preserve. To help achieve a set, sugar with pectin is used, or liquid pectin is added. The mixture is then boiled for about 4 minutes before testing for setting point (see page 17). Freezer jam must be kept in the refrigerator after thawing.

JELLY a softly firm preserve. By convention, jellies should be crystal clear, but the clarity depends on slow, undisturbed straining of the cooked, unsweetened fruit. The amount of water used affects the strength of flavour of the prepared jelly.
WATCHPOINTS see *Making Jellies* (pages 16-17)

Below, from left to right: Plum Jelly, Seville Orange Marmalade, Strawberry Conserve, Pecan and Whisky Mincemeat, Lemon Curd.

MARMALADE a sweet preserve based on citrus fruits. Seville oranges make the best marmalades; sweet oranges tend to give a more cloudy appearance and their pith does not become translucent. Marmalades can be chunky, thin-cut or fine-shred.
WATCHPOINTS see *Making Marmalades* (pages 18-19)

CONSERVE made from whole or chopped fruit suspended in a thick or lightly gelled syrup. The fruit, which must be completely dry, is layered with sugar and left overnight to coax the juices out and keep the fruit firm. The subsequent brief boiling draws out more juices, often making it unnecessary to add any water. The short cooking time preserves the fruity, fresh flavour.
WATCHPOINTS see *Making Jams* (pages 14-15)

FRUIT BUTTER a soft, thick, spreadable mixture of sieved fruit purée and sugar. The texture is determined by consistency rather than by set or temperature. The fruit is cooked with a minimum of water until soft, then it is puréed and sieved through a non-metallic sieve; 225-350g/8-12oz sugar is added to every 450g/1lb fruit pulp and the mixture is heated gently, then boiled for 30-45 minutes until the butter has the consistency of thick double cream. Stir the mixture occasionally to start, then more frequently as the cooking progresses. To test for correct consistency, put a spoonful on a cold plate; if water seeps out the butter is not thick enough and should be cooked for longer.
WATCHPOINTS for making fruit butter
Caramelized butter: the purée was too thin before the sugar was added and before sufficient water had evaporated.
Thin, flavourless butter: the butter was insufficiently cooked and may ferment on storage. Boil a little longer to thicken.

FRUIT CHEESE a fruit butter that has been cooked for 45-55 minutes until it is so thick that it sets firmly enough to be sliced. Fruit cheeses can be set in decorative moulds.
WATCHPOINTS see *Fruit Butter*

FRUIT CURD made from egg yolks or whole eggs, sugar and fruit or fruit juice. Use fresh, free-range eggs and unsalted butter.
WATCHPOINTS for making fruit curd
Curdling eggs: the bottom of the basin touched the water during cooking; the water was boiling rather than simmering. To remedy, transfer the basin immediately to a bowl of cold water and beat the curd hard. Strain through a non-metallic sieve and start again, adding another egg.

𝒯YPES OF 𝒫RESERVE

MINCEMEAT this was originally made with minced meat. Nowadays, the meat has been replaced by shredded beef suet. Vegetarian suets are also available.
WATCHPOINTS for making mincemeat
Fermentation: there is insufficient sugar, fruit, acid or alcohol in the mincemeat; the jars are not clean. Rectify by reboiling the mincemeat (although it may soften and the flavour may be affected).
Drying of the surface: the mincemeat was not covered properly. Stir in a little of the alcohol used in the recipe and re-cover.

FRUITS IN ALCOHOL raw or lightly cooked fruit is steeped in alcohol. Any spirit or liqueur of least 40 per cent alcohol (80 per cent proof) will be effective. Wines and fortified wines need to be combined with another means of preservation, usually sugar.
WATCHPOINTS for making fruits in alcohol
Fruit rises to the top of the jar: weight down with crumpled greaseproof paper. Remove after 1 week and top up with alcohol.

CANDIED, CRYSTALLIZED AND GLACE FRUITS a selection of fruits are impregnated with sugar over a period of about 3 weeks and then left for the surface to dry out.
WATCHPOINTS see *Making Candied Fruits* (pages 20-21)

Below, from left to right: Quince Cheese, Tomato Ketchup, Dill Pickled Gherkins, Mango Chutney and Beetroot and Horseradish Relish.

CHUTNEY a sweet-sour mixture of finely chopped vegetables and fruit, cooked with spices or herbs, vinegar and sugar. You can use damaged vegetables if you remove the affected parts but avoid mouldy produce. Fruit should not be over-ripe. Thick-skinned fruit or vegetables should be cooked first in the vinegar to soften them. The fruit or vegetables are cooked slowly with the remaining ingredients until the mixture is smooth and thick with no free liquid. The chutney should be stirred frequently.
WATCHPOINTS for making chutney
Dry, brown surface: the cover is not airtight; the storage place is too warm.
Fermenting or mouldy chutney: the storage place is too warm; there is insufficient vinegar or sugar; the chutney is too thin; the jars or lids are dirty.

RELISH similar to a chutney but containing larger pieces of vegetable or fruit. Relishes have a shorter cooking time.
WATCHPOINTS *see Chutney*

SAUCE bottled sauces were popular with the Victorians and Edwardians. The word 'ketchup' comes from the Far East and traditionally was applied to thin, salty sauces. After cooking in a spiced vinegar, the vegetables or fruit are sieved or puréed, then simmered to a creamy consistency.
WATCHPOINTS for making sauces
Thin sauce: the sauce was not boiled for long enough and may go off.

PICKLE raw or lightly cooked vegetables or fruit are preserved in clear, spiced vinegar. Raw vegetables are usually salted before being pickled, either with dry salt (for wet vegetables such as cucumbers) or in brine. Salting draws out excess moisture which would dilute the vinegar and shorten the storage time. Salted vegetables must be rinsed under cold running water, then drained and dried thoroughly. Cooked vegetables do not need brining, but should be dried thoroughly before cooking. Fruit is lightly cooked in sweetened spiced vinegar; the vinegar can be boiled to make a syrup.
WATCHPOINTS for making pickles
Mouldy pickle: the brining solution was not strong enough; the vinegar was too weak; the jars were not clean; the vegetables are not covered by vinegar.
Cloudy vinegar: the brining was not done for long enough; ground spices were used.

VEGETABLES IN OIL surplus water must be removed from vegetables first by cooking them. Choose vegetables that are in good condition and use fresh oil. I use a mild olive oil because it adds a richness of flavour (it is a good idea to open a new bottle).
WATCHPOINTS for making vegetables in oil
Rancid oil: the storage place is too warm or light; the oil was not fresh.
Mouldy or discoloured vegetables at the top of the jar: the vegetables have not been completely covered in oil; surplus water was not removed from them.

E QUIPMENT

PAN a traditional preserving pan (maslin) with sloping sides, a pouring lip and carrying handle is useful but not essential (the recipes in this book are for fairly small amounts).

The pan should not be more than half-full when cooking sweetened mixtures as they spit in hot explosions when boiled. It should provide a large surface area to enable unwanted water to steam and evaporate rapidly; if you are boiling a fairly small quantity of a savoury sauce, you can use a large non-stick frying pan.

Make sure your pan is not pitted or damaged in any way. The base should be flat and heavy so that heat is conducted evenly and mixtures do not catch and burn on the bottom of the pan. Stainless steel pans are often recommended but aluminium pans with non-stick linings are fine. Unlined copper or brass pans should not be used unless specified. Two handles opposite each other make for easier lifting.

KNIVES stainless steel knives prevent discoloration of fruit and vegetables.

FOOD PROCESSOR this cuts down the time it takes to prepare vegetables and fruit peels.

LONG-HANDLED WOODEN SPOONS use for all stirring, especially hot mixtures and those containing acid (a metal spoon may react with the acid and discolour the ingredients).

SLOTTED SPOON OR SKIMMER for skimming scum and removing stones from hot mixtures.

SIEVES AND COLANDERS use heatproof plastic or nylon. These are essential for use with ingredients containing acid.

NON-METALLIC BOWLS necessary when using ingredients containing acid.

CALIBRATED HEATPROOF JUG essential for measuring and pouring hot mixtures.

WIDE-NECKED NON-METALLIC FUNNEL with a non-stick surface for pouring liquids from one container into another without spilling.

JELLY BAG a wind-sock shaped bag, usually nylon, is used when making jellies. Jelly bags are often sold with their own stand, but can easily be fixed to the legs of an upturned stool, or suspended from a wire coat hanger hanging from a peg. A non-metallic bowl placed beneath the bag will catch the drips. A jelly bag can be improvised by tying a double thickness of muslin, cheesecloth or fine cloth to the legs of an upturned stool. Always scald the jelly bag before use.

MUSLIN BAG to enclose spices or pips so they can be removed before potting. Use muslin, cheesecloth or fine cloth. Tie the bag to the pan handle with string long enough for it to be suspended in the preserve.

LADLE for transferring preserves from the pan to the containers without spilling.

TONGS for lifting hot bottles and jars.

JARS AND BOTTLES scrutinize them carefully to make sure there are no cracks, chips or other flaws. If a hot mixture is added to a flawed jar, the jar will immediately shatter. Bacteria can breed in small cracks, which could cause your preserve to go off.

For processing in a waterbath (see page 13) you will need special jars with lids that are held in place by screw-bands or clips.
Preparing jars and bottles: wash well in hot soapy water, then rinse in hot water and put into a preheated oven at 140°C/275°F/gas mark 1 for 30 minutes. Use warm jars when

filling hot preserves to prevent cracking, but leave to cool when filling with cold preserves.

COVERS AND LIDS use waxed discs, applied waxed-side down, to cover the surface of preserves that are not liquid or not processed in a waterbath. To cover the container, use cellophane covers or a double thickness of cling film pulled taut. Secure the cover with string or elastic bands in

ℰQUIPMENT

good condition. Screw-top lids must be vinegar-proof or have a vinegar-proof lining.

If you re-use screw-top lids, boil them for 10 minutes, then drain them and tip into a colander. Leave to dry naturally. Corks should be new and boiled for 10 minutes to expand them and to ensure they are clean.

LABELS these should have a good adhesive backing and plenty of space for recording important information.

PRESSURE COOKERS a cooker with a three-pressure gauge saves time and fruit retains its flavour and colour. It can be used for the preliminary softening of the fruit, peel or vegetables. Consult the manufacturer's handbook for recipes and timings. General points to remember are:

1 Remove the trivet from the pan (except for bottling, when it is used upside down).
2 The pan should not be more than half-full.
3 When making jams, jellies and marmalades cook the fruit at 10lb pressure (medium). Pectin will be destroyed if cooked at 15lb pressure (high).
4 Reduce the pressure at room temperature before opening.

MICROWAVE COOKERS can be used for preparing small amounts of preserves such as jams, curds and relishes. Always use a large bowl that is no more than one-third full, to avoid boiling over.

Below, from left to right: tongs, ladle, preserving pan, nylon sieve, sharp stainless steel knife, stainless steel saucepan, sugar thermometer with clip, slotted spoon, jelly bag, wooden spoons, pyrex bowl, funnel with non-stick lining.

FILLING AND COVERING

Fill the containers cleanly so there are no sticky spills down the sides. Wipe the rims and sides with a hot, soapy cloth then dry thoroughly with a clean cloth. With the exception of products that are processed in a waterbath, fill containers to within 1.25cm/½in of the top.

All hot preserves should be covered with air-tight lids within about 20 minutes. As the preserve cools, so does the air beneath the lid, contracting to create a partial vacuum, which helps to protect the preserve from spoilage. If you have to delay covering the preserve, wait until it is completely cold. If it is covered while lukewarm, the trapped moisture and warmth provide the perfect breeding ground for bacteria and moulds.

Jams and conserves: strawberry jams and conserves should always be left to stand off the heat for 10-15 minutes to prevent the fruit from rising to the top. For other preserves, see individual recipes (whether preserves are left to stand or not depends on the density of the fruit and the amount used). If in doubt, leave to stand. Ladle into warm, clean, dry jars through a funnel, then cover with waxed discs, waxed-side down and seal tightly.

Marmalades: leave to stand (see individual recipes). Fill, cover and seal as for jams.

Jellies, fruit butters, cheeses and curds: these can be potted immediately (leave jellies to stand if they contain herbs or other

𝓕ILLING AND 𝓒OVERING

particles). Fill, cover and seal as for jams. To mould a cheese, brush the mould lightly first with flavourless oil or glycerine.

Mincemeat: leave overnight before potting. When filling jars, make sure you pack in the mincemeat firmly, leaving no air pockets. Cover and seal as for jams.

Chutneys, relishes: pour while still hot into warm, clean dry jars, making sure there are no air pockets. Cover with a waxed disc, waxed-side down, then close with air-tight, vinegar-proof lids or cellophane covers.

Sauces and drinks: fill containers or bottles while still hot and cover with vinegar-proof screw-top lids or ground glass stoppers.

Pickles: pack the fruit or vegetables into clean, dry jars to within 1.25cm/½in of the top, adding any spices as you go; take care when packing cooked vegetables not to spoil their shape. Pour over the vinegar syrup, or vinegar (hot for soft pickles such as peaches and prunes, cold for hard ones such as onions) so the vegetables are well covered but do not allow the vinegar to come into contact with the lid. Swivel the jar to dispel any trapped air bubbles. Cover with a vinegar-proof lid and seal.

Vegetables in oil, fruits in alcohol: the vegetables or fruits should be completely covered by oil or alcohol; swivel the jar to expel any trapped air bubbles. Cover fruits in alcohol with vinegar-proof lids and do not allow the alcohol to touch the lid. Seal.

LABELLING although it may seem obvious to you what is in a jar when you have just made it, after a while the contents can become just a faded memory. Be sure to label all containers, not just with the contents but also the date they were made and any special usage or storage information.

STORAGE AND SHELF-LIFE all preserves should be kept in a cool, dark, dry place.

Jams, jellies, marmalades, conserves: will keep for up to 1 year.

Fruit butters: will keep for up to 3 months.

Fruit cheeses: because they are so concentrated, cheeses will keep for up to, or even beyond, a year.

Curds: will keep for 4-6 weeks in a cool place or up to 3 months in the refrigerator.

Mincemeat: will keep for 12-18 months.

Chutneys, relishes: will keep for 1 year or more if properly stored.

Sauces: home-made sauces with low quantities of vinegar or salt should be processed in a waterbath to extend their shelf-life. See individual recipes.

Drinks: if spirit-based, will keep for 3-5 years.

Pickles: will keep for 1 year or more.

Vegetables in oil: will keep for 9-12 months.

Fruits in alcohol: will keep for 2 years or more if properly stored.

Candied, crystallized and glacé fruits: will keep for up to 2 years, if not longer.

PROCESSING IN A WATERBATH this is a very straightforward way of extending the shelf-life of bottled fruit and other preserves. Air is expelled during processing, creating a partial vacuum in the container. A tight seal is formed, preventing the sterilized contents from becoming contaminated. Use flawless jars with screw bands or spring clips.

Covering hot preserves: cover the entire surface with a waxed disc, waxed-side down. Cover with dampened cellophane and secure with string.

Processing fruit: prepare the fruit and cook as required. Pack the fruit firmly into warm, clean, dry jars. Put 225g/8oz sugar in a saucepan with 300ml/10fl oz water and heat gently, stirring, until the sugar has dissolved. Bring to the boil for 1 minute without stirring. Add 270ml/9fl oz water and return to the boil. If the syrup is not used immediately, cover the pan. The syrup can be flavoured with whole spices, freshly grated ginger or spirits. Pour boiling syrup over the fruit to cover, leaving a headspace of 1.25cm/½in to allow for expansion.

Swivel the jar to expel air bubbles then cover loosely. If using jars with screw-bands, loosen the bands by half a turn. Stand the jars on a trivet or thick pad of newspaper in a deep pan (make sure they are not touching each other or the sides of the pan). Pour in warm water to cover by at least 2.5cm/1in. Bring the water temperature to 88°C/190°F in 25-30 minutes. Maintain this temperature for the specified length of time (see below). Using tongs, transfer the jars to a wooden surface and tighten the lids. Leave until completely cold, then test the seals. Remove the screw bands or spring clips and lift each bottle by the lid. If a vacuum has been formed, the lid will hold. If a seal has not been obtained, the contents of the jar or bottle should be used straight away. Store in a cool, dark, dry place.

Processing times (1 litre/2 pint jars): *blackberries, currants, loganberries, mulberries, raspberries, gooseberries:* 2 minutes (normal pack), 10 minutes (tight pack); *apricots (whole), cherries, damsons, greengages and plums:* 10 minutes; *apricots, nectarines, peaches, plums (all halved):* 20 minutes; *whole small peeled peaches:* 20 minutes at 100°C/212°F.

Sauces and Drinks: pour the hot sauce or drink into warm, clean, dry bottles, leaving a headspace of 1.25cm/½in. Put on the clean lids but do not secure tightly. Process the bottles as above. See individual recipes for times.

ℳAKING ℐAMS

It is best to use fruit that is not quite ripe for making jams, as this will contain the most pectin. The amount of sugar that is added will vary according to the sugar content of the fruit (classically, the sugar represents 60-65% of the total weight of a finished jam). The longer the fruit takes to cook the greater the amount of water that is added. The fruit can be gently crushed against the bottom of the pan to hasten the release of the juices (do not crush strawberries as the pieces should be left whole). The recipe below can be adapted by adding flavourings such as orange flower or rose water, gin, brandy, eau-de-vie or kirsch. Stir in two tablespoons of the flavouring just before potting.

Strawberry Jam

MAKES 1.8KG/4LB

900g/2lb strawberries
juice of ½ lemon
900g/2lb sugar with pectin, warmed
 (see page 7)
15g/½oz butter (optional)

EQUIPMENT
- **Sharp stainless steel kitchen knives**
- **Chopping board**
- **Preserving pan or very large non-aluminium**
  saucepan
- **Long-handled wooden spoon**
- **Sugar thermometer (optional)**
- **Saucer**
- **Teaspoon**
- **Slotted spoon**
- **Funnel**
- **Suitable jam jars, wax discs, and lids or covers**

1 Prepare the strawberries by hulling and halving them with a sharp knife. Place them in a preserving pan with the lemon juice and add 4 tablespoons of water. Gently warm the contents of the pan over a low heat for 3-4 minutes.

2 Add the warmed sugar with pectin to the pan and cook very gently over a low heat, stirring the mixture carefully, until all the sugar has dissolved.

Making Jams

3 A knob of butter can be added to the jam after adding the sugar, to reduce scum formation. Put the saucer to chill.

WATCHPOINTS

Cloudy jam: *the fruit was damaged or not clean.*

Crystallized, grainy jam: *the jam was boiled before all the sugar had dissolved completely. To rectify, boil the jam, adding a little water or alcohol such as brandy, whisky or a liqueur, then repot.*

Dark, runny jam: *the jam was overboiled beyond the setting point.*

Jam that does not set or is syrupy: *the jam was not boiled for long enough (rectify by reboiling to reach setting point); there was insufficient pectin in the fruit (rectify by adding liquid pectin to the finished jam or use more lemon juice before first boiling).*

Jam that ferments on storage: *the jam was not boiled for long enough. Fermented jams*

are harmless and can be reboiled so they reach setting point; reboiling may spoil the flavour and colour of the jam.

Hard, dry jam with poor colour and flavour: *the jam was boiled for too long; it has been stored in a warm or damp place.*

Mouldy jam: *the jars were cold or damp or they were underfilled; if there was a delay in covering the jam with a waxed disc, the surface may have been infected by mould spores in the air which have now grown on the jam; the jam has been stored in a warm or damp place.*

Air pockets: *the jam was too cool when it was poured into the jars.*

Fruit rises to the top of the jam: *the jam was not left to stand for 10-15 minutes before potting.*

4 Raise the heat and boil the jam hard, without stirring, until setting point is reached. This should take about 4 minutes (for recipes using ordinary sugar, test after 10-15 minutes). To test for set, remove the pan from the heat and drop a little jam on to the cold saucer. Push it gently with the tip of a teaspoon or your finger. If the surface wrinkles, setting point has been reached. Alternatively, test with a sugar thermometer (see page 17).

5 Skim any scum from the surface of the jam using a slotted spoon. Leave to stand for 10-15 minutes before potting so that the fruit does not rise to the top, but is evenly distributed throughout the jam when the jars are filled.

6 Ladle the jam into warm, clean, dry jars almost to the top through a funnel. Immediately cover the entire surface of the jam with waxed discs, waxed-side down and smooth down with the fingertip. The disc should cover the surface of the jam completely. Cover with a dampened cellophane circle and secure in place with string. Leave overnight to cool and set slightly. Store in a cool, dry, dark place.

Making Jellies

Jellies are often more versatile than jams, as they can be served with savoury as well as sweet dishes. For sparkling, crystal-clear jellies the fruit mixture must be strained through a special jelly bag (see page 10), which can take anything from eight to twelve hours. If you are not concerned about clarity, the time can be reduced by using a sieve lined with a double thickness of muslin and, if you are really pushed for time, by lightly squeezing the fruit in the sieve. The recipe below shows the basic method of jelly-making, but also explains how you can incorporate herbs and other flavourings during the cooking process. Use it as a reference when making the jellies in this book.

Orange and Tarragon Jelly

MAKES 1.4-1.5KG/3-3½LB

1.4kg/3lb oranges, sliced
350g/12oz lemons, sliced
4 tablespoons chopped tarragon
warmed sugar (see page 7)

EQUIPMENT
- Sharp stainless steel kitchen knives
- Chopping board
- Measuring jug
- Scales
- Preserving pan or large non-aluminium saucepan
- Long-handled wooden spoon
- Jelly bag, or a large piece of fine cotton, or enough muslin to make a three-times thickness
- Upturned stool or other method of supporting the jelly bag
- Sugar thermometer (optional)
- Saucer
- Teaspoon
- Slotted spoon
- Funnel
- Suitable jam jars, wax discs, and lids or covers

1 Chop the fruit slices and put them in a pan with 2.1 litres/3¾ pints water and half the tarragon. Bring to the boil, then simmer gently, stirring occasionally with a wooden spoon to prevent sticking, for about 1¼ hours, until soft.

2 Scald the jelly bag – or cotton or muslin, whichever you are using – by pouring boiling water through it. Tie the bag or cloth to the legs of an upturned stool and stand a large non-metallic or stainless steel bowl underneath the jelly bag. Tip the contents of the pan into the bag or cloth and leave to strain, undisturbed, in a cool place for 8-12 hours, until the liquid has stopped dripping through.

Making Jellies

3 Measure the juice collected in the bowl and pour it back into the rinsed-out pan. Add 450g/1lb warmed sugar for every 570ml/1pint juice. Heat gently, stirring, until the sugar has completely dissolved, then raise the heat and boil hard until the setting point is reached. Do not allow gas flames to lick up the sides of the pan. Stir the juice occasionally to make sure the jelly cooks evenly and to prevent sticking.

WATCHPOINTS

Cloudy jelly: *the fruit was damaged or not clean; the jelly bag was not clean; the jelly bag was squeezed or pressed while the juice was being strained through the bag.*
Grainy crystallized sugar: *the strained juice was boiled before all the sugar had completely dissolved.*
Syrupy, dark jelly that will not set: *the jelly was overboiled beyond the setting point.*
Watery jelly that will not set: *the jelly was not boiled for long enough; rectify by reboiling the jelly.*
Mouldy jelly: *the jars were cold or damp or they were underfilled; the jelly has not been stored in a cool, dark, dry place.*
See also Making Jams (pages 14-15)

4 A jam thermometer lets you know how boiling is proceeding: clip the thermometer on to the side of the pan if you can, or hold it for a short while well down in the boiling jelly, but away from the bottom of the pan. Most jellies set at 105°C/221°F, but some fruits may need a degree higher or lower, so it is worth double-checking with a saucer test.

5 To test for set, put a saucer to chill before starting the second boiling. When ready to test, remove the pan from the heat and drop a little jelly on to the cold saucer. Push it gently with the tip of a teaspoon or your finger: if the surface wrinkles, setting point has been reached.

6 With the pan off the heat, remove any scum from the surface with a slotted spoon, then stir in the remaining tarragon. Leave the jelly to stand for 10-15 minutes. Have some clean, dry, warm jars standing ready. Ladle the jelly in through a funnel and fill each jar to the top. Wipe the rim of the jars with a warm, damp cloth, then put a waxed disc on top of the jelly, waxed-side down, making sure it lies completely flat. Cover and seal the jars. Leave overnight to set. Store in a cool, dark, dry place.

Making Marmalades

Marmalades are made in much the same way as jams. They can be chunky, thin-cut or fine shred depending on how the peel is prepared. The initial cooking time is often longer because citrus peels are thicker than fruit skins, so they take longer to soften. Seville oranges are, of course, the king of the marmalade fruits and they are grown in Spain almost exclusively for export for British marmalade making. They come on to the market in January and early February and I always hungrily buy vast amounts. What I don't get round to using straight away I put into plastic bags and freeze for later (pectin deteriorates with time, so add 1 extra orange per 450g/1lb).

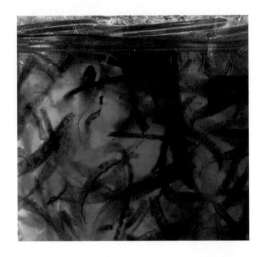

Seville Orange Marmalade

MAKES ABOUT 2.5KG/5LB

675g/1½lb Seville oranges
juice of 1 large lemon
1.4kg/3lb sugar

EQUIPMENT
- Sharp stainless steel kitchen knives
- Chopping board
- Lemon squeezer
- Small piece of muslin
- Kitchen string
- Preserving pan or very large non-aluminium saucepan
- Slotted spoon
- Wooden spoon
- Saucer
- Sugar thermometer (optional)
- Funnel
- Suitable jam jars, wax discs, and lids or covers

1 Cut the oranges in half and squeeze out all the juice, reserving the pips and any membrane that comes away during squeezing.

2 Place the pips and membrane on a piece of muslin. Tie into a bag with a long length of string.

*M*AKING *M*ARMALADES

WATCHPOINTS
Tough peel: *the peel was not cooked for long enough before adding the sugar.*
Peel rises to the top of the jar: *the marmalade was not left to stand for 10-15 minutes before being potted.*
Shrinkage on storage: *the marmalade was not covered correctly; the wax disc does not cover the entire surface of the marmalade; the marmalade has not been kept in a cool, dark, dry place.*
See also Making Jams (pages 14-15)

3 Slice the orange peel as required and put into a pan with the orange and lemon juices and 1.7 litres/3 pints water.

4 Tie the string to the pan handle so the bag is suspended in the mixture. Bring to the boil then simmer for 1-1½ hours.

5 At the end of the boiling time, the peel should be soft and the liquid reduced by half. Scoop out the muslin bag with a slotted spoon and squeeze it hard against the side of the pan so the juice runs back into the pan. Discard the bag.

Place a saucer to chill ready for testing for a set.

6 Over a low heat, stir the sugar into the marmalade using a wooden spoon, until the sugar is dissolved. Raise the heat and boil hard for 10-15 minutes, stirring as necessary, until setting point has been reached. Test for setting point by placing a spoonful of marmalade on to the chilled saucer. If the surface of the marmalade wrinkles when pushed with a spoon, setting point has been reached. Alternatively, use a sugar thermometer (see page 17).

7 Remove the pan from the heat and skim the scum from the surface with a slotted spoon. Leave to stand for 10-15 minutes then stir and ladle into warm, clean, dry jars. Cover and seal (see pages 12-13). Leave overnight. Store in a cool, dark, dry place.

Variations: *Orange Whisky Marmalade* Add 150ml/5fl oz whisky after skimming the marmalade; *Ginger Marmalade:* peel and shred 150g/5oz fresh ginger, and add to the marmalade with the fruit peels.

Making Candied Fruits

Good candied, crystallized and glacé fruit is expensive to buy but can be prepared at home without much difficulty. The process may seem rather long-winded, but the results are worth the effort. Use firm, ripe, undamaged fruit.

For plums, greengages, apricots, kumquats: prick all over with a needle so the syrup penetrates evenly and right throught to the centre. For cherries: remove the stones using a cherry stoner. For citrus fruits (except kumquats): peel and divide into segments, removing all the skin and pith. For pears, apples and peaches: peel, then halve or thickly slice. For pineapple: remove the skin, 'eyes' and core; cut into chunks or rings.

Candied fruit: for each 450g/1lb fruit, you will need 625g/1lb 6oz sugar
Crystallized fruit: for each 450g/1lb candied fruit, you will need about 225g/8oz caster sugar
Glacé fruit: for each 450g/1lb candied fruit, you will need 450g/1lb sugar

EQUIPMENT
For candied fruit:
- **Needle, cherry stoner or sharp kitchen knives**
- **Kitchen scales**
- **2 saucepans**
- **Slotted spoon**
- **Wire basket to fit inside second saucepan**
- **Measuring jug**
- **Wooden spoon**
- **Wire rack**
- **Kitchen foil**
In addition (for crystallized fruit):
- **Skewer**
- **Small bowl**
- **Baking tray**
(for glacé fruit):
- **2 saucepans (1 large and 1 small)**
- **Cup or small bowl**
- **Skewer**
Plus suitable boxes or containers, waxed paper

1 Weigh the fruit after it has been prepared. Put the fruit in a saucepan, add just enough boiling water to cover, then simmer gently, covered, until tender – soft fruits take only 2-3 minutes, firm ones such as apricots, 10-15 minutes. Using a slotted spoon, carefully transfer the fruit to a wire basket placed inside another saucepan.

2 Measure 300ml/10fl oz of the cooking water for every 450g/1lb prepared weight of fruit. Now make the sugar syrup. In a saucepan, gently heat 175g/6oz sugar (to every 450g/1lb prepared weight of fruit) with the measured cooking water, stirring with a wooden spoon until the sugar has dissolved. Raise the heat and bring the liquid to the boil.

Making Candied Fruits

3 Pour the hot syrup over the fruit, cover and leave for 1 day in a cool place. The next day, lift out the basket with the fruit.

4 Add another 50g/2oz sugar to the syrup and dissolve over a low heat, stirring. Raise the heat, bring to the boil, then remove from the heat and lower the fruit into the pan once more. Cover and leave in a cool place for 1 day. Repeat this step daily for the next 5 days so the syrup gradually becomes more concentrated.

5 Lift the basket containing the fruit from the saucepan, add 75g/3oz sugar to the syrup and heat gently, stirring, until the sugar has dissolved. Lower the fruit back into the pan and simmer gently for 3-4 minutes. Remove from the heat, cover and leave in a cool place for 2 days. Repeat this step once more, but leave the fruit to stand for 4 days or up to 2 weeks.

6 Lift the wire basket containing the fruit from the sugar syrup for the last time and, using a pair of tongs, transfer each piece of fruit on to a wire rack placed over a tray, to dry. Protect the fruit from dust by placing a dome of kitchen foil over the wire rack making sure that it does not touch the surface of the fruit. Leave the fruit in a warm, dry place for 2-3 days, turning each piece over two or three times, until it is completely dry.

Using a pair of tongs, carefully pack the fruit into attractive boxes or other containers, placing waxed paper between each layer. If you have used an assortment of fruits, you can either layer them according to type or mix the fruit together for an attractive, colourful presentation.

Crystallized Fruit

To make crystallized fruits you have to candy them first (see above). Fill a small bowl with caster sugar and bring a saucepan of water to the boil. Spear each piece of completely dry candied fruit with a skewer and quickly dip it in the boiling water. Allow any excess moisture to drain off then roll the fruit in the caster sugar. Transfer to a foil-lined tray and leave to dry.

Glacé Fruit

Candied fruits are also the starting point for glacé fruits. Heat 150ml/5fl oz water with the sugar and stir until the sugar has dissolved. Boil for 1 minute. Pour a little hot syrup into a warm bowl. Cover the syrup in the pan and place in a saucepan of simmering water to keep warm. Spear each piece of fruit with a skewer, dip into boiling water for 20 seconds then dip into the syrup.

As each piece of fruit is ready, transfer it to a wire rack placed over a tray. As the syrup in the cup becomes cloudy, discard it and add fresh hot syrup.

Cover the fruit with a dome of kitchen foil. Leave to dry in a warm place for 2-3 days, turning a few times.

WATCHPOINTS
Shapeless or tough fruit: *the soft fruit was cooked for too long at the beginning.*

$\mathcal{V}$EGETABLES

This chapter contains an enormous range and variety of vegetable preserves from modest Pickled Baby Beetroot (see page 26) to the more upmarket Artichokes in Oil (see page 24), Angel's Hair (see page 27) and fashionable Grilled Red Peppers in Oil (see page 32), which come into their own in a delicious Fettucine with Smoked Trout, Basil and Grilled Red Peppers (see page 33). Preserved vegetables are real storecupboard stalwarts. With this imaginative and mouthwatering selection of recipes you need never be at a loss for a snack, a starter, a vegetable accompaniment, or something unusual to boost a main course or liven up a salad, picnic or buffet.

Left (from left to right): Italian Garden Pickle, Artichokes in Oil, Ratatouille Chutney and Spiced Green Olives.

Artichokes in Oil

If you are able to find very small artichokes, preserve them whole, as the Italians do.

MAKES 1 LITRE/1¾ PINTS

1.4kg/3lb globe artichokes
½ lemon
1 litre/1¾ pints white wine vinegar
500ml/18fl oz dry white wine
3 sprigs of fresh thyme
1 small sprig of fresh rosemary
6 garlic cloves
about 850ml/1½ pints olive oil
2 dried red chillies (optional)
sea salt

Snap the stalks from the artichokes and trim away the outer leaves. Trim the tops of the leaves, then cut the artichokes into halves or quarters. Cut out the hairy chokes. Drop the artichokes into a bowl of water acidulated with a good squeeze of lemon juice.

Add the vinegar, wine, 2 sprigs of thyme and the rosemary to a large saucepan, then bring to the boil.

Tie the garlic in a square of muslin and add to the pan for several seconds. Fish out and reserve the bag.

Add the artichokes to the pan and cook for about 20 minutes or until tender. Drain them and leave to dry on paper towels.

Pour a thin layer of oil into a preserving jar. Add a layer of artichokes, using a spoon; pack them in well so no air is trapped. Pour in more oil, add a garlic clove and a little crumbled chilli, if using, then repeat the layering. Insert the remaining thyme to the side of the jar when it is partly filled. Cover the artichokes with oil before sealing the jar (see pages 12-13). Store in a cool, dark, dry place for at least 2 months before eating.

Toss with chopped parsley, a squeeze of lemon juice, black pepper, chopped dried red chilli and a little olive oil.

Artichoke and Mushroom Pizza

Use a combination of Artichokes in Oil and oyster mushrooms to transform a bought pizza base.

SERVES 2

115g/4oz oyster mushrooms, sliced
350g/12oz Artichokes in Oil (see left)
2-3 tablespoons oil from the artichokes
squeeze of lemon juice
25cm/10in prepared pizza base
75-115g/3-4oz fontina cheese, grated
sea salt and freshly ground black pepper
chopped fresh thyme for sprinkling

Preheat the oven to 220°C/425°F/gas mark 7.

Sauté the mushrooms in a little of the artichoke oil, then toss them with the artichokes.

Mix a squeeze of lemon juice with the remaining artichoke oil and brush over the pizza base. Distribute the artichokes and mushrooms evenly over the base, then scatter the cheese over the top. Bake for about 20 minutes, or according to instructions on the pizza base packet. Sprinkle with thyme and serve.

Below: Artichoke and Mushroom Pizza. You can add more artichokes and mushrooms for an extra generous topping.

$\mathscr{A}$UBERGINES

Aubergine and Pepper Pickle

MAKES ABOUT 1KG/2¼LB

450g/1lb aubergines
sea salt
4 large red peppers, or 2 red and 2 yellow
  peppers
300ml/10fl oz white wine vinegar
1-2 garlic cloves, cut into slivers
6 anchovy fillets, drained
2-3 teaspoons capers, preferably salt-packed,
  drained
1 teaspoon black peppercorns
several basil leaves
about 300ml/10fl oz olive oil

Preheat the grill to high. Cut the aubergines in half lengthways, then cut into 0.5cm/¼in slices. Layer the slices in a non-metallic colander, sprinkling each layer with salt. Leave to drain for 2-3 hours.

Meanwhile, grill the peppers until the skins are charred and blistered. Leave until they are cool enough to handle, then peel them. Discard the cores and seeds and cut the flesh into 0.5cm/¼in strips.

Rinse the aubergines well under running cold water, then drain and dry them thoroughly on paper towels.

Bring the vinegar and 150ml/5fl oz water to the boil in a large saucepan, add the aubergines and garlic and blanch for 1 minute. Drain well.

Pour a little oil into a warm, clean, dry 1kg/2¼lb jar, then layer the aubergines, garlic and peppers in the jar, adding an anchovy fillet, 2 or 3 capers, 1-2 peppercorns and a basil leaf here and there. Add more oil between the layers. Cover completely with olive oil and swivel the jar to make sure all the air is expelled, then cover and seal (see pages 12-13). Store in a cool, dark, dry place for at least 1 month before eating.

Middle Eastern Stuffed Aubergines in Oil

Pickles are very popular in the Middle East. Many families still prepare large glass jars (*martabans*) filled with vegetables and colourful displays are a common sight in shop windows.

MAKES 750ML/1½ PINTS

900g/2lb small aubergines
sea salt
4 garlic cloves, finely chopped
1-2 small dried red chillies, seeded and finely
  chopped
leaves from several sprigs of fresh coriander
  or parsley
about 250-300ml/8-10fl oz olive oil

Cut off the stem ends of the aubergines. Make a small slit in the middle of each aubergine then place them in a large pan of salted water and poach over a low heat for about 20 minutes until they are tender; keep the aubergines submerged with a heavy lid that will fit inside the pan.

Drain the aubergines and leave them until they are cool enough to handle, then squeeze them to remove the juices.

Stuffing aubergines: use a sharp knife to ease the chilli mixture into each aubergine for Middle Eastern Stuffed Aubergines in Oil.

Mix together the garlic, chillies, coriander or parsley and a pinch of salt.

Enlarge the slit in each aubergine and insert some of the chilli mixture (see below).

Pack the aubergines into a clean, dry jar and pour in oil to cover. Cover and seal (see pages 12-13). Store in a cool, dark, dry place for 2-4 weeks before opening.

Aubergine, Okra and Coriander Relish

Choose small, unblemished, completely green okra for this fragrant relish.

MAKES ABOUT 1.25KG/2¾LB

450g/1lb aubergines, cut into thick chunks
4 teaspoons sea salt
1 large onion, coarsely chopped
2 garlic cloves, crushed
2 celery stalks, coarsely chopped
225g/8oz small okra, sliced
2 tablespoons tomato purée
1-2 tablespoons curry powder, to taste
2 teaspoons ground allspice
1 teaspoon ground ginger
115g/4oz soft brown sugar
1.1 litres/2 pints white wine vinegar
2 tablespoons chopped fresh coriander

Layer the aubergines and salt in a non-metallic colander. Leave to drain overnight.

Dry but do not rinse the aubergines, then put into a pan with the other ingredients, except the coriander. Simmer for 30 minutes, stir in the coriander, then pack into warm, clean, dry jars. Cover with vinegar-proof lids and seal (see pages 12-13). Store in a cool, dark, dry place for 2-4 weeks before eating.

Serve as an accompaniment to an Indian meal, or with good bread and cheese.

Pickled Baby Beetroot

Choose baby beetroot with undamaged and blemish-free skins, and do not peel them until after they have been cooked, otherwise the colour will 'bleed'. Most pickles are bottled cold but because of the size of the beetroot in this recipe, the jars are filled when the ingredients are still hot.

MAKES ABOUT 900G/2LB

900g/2lb baby beetroot, left whole
1-1½ teaspoons sugar
2 teaspoons salt
570ml/1 pint Spiced Vinegar (see page 139), made with red wine vinegar
allspice berries

Cook the beetroot in boiling water for 30-40 minutes until tender. Drain and rinse the beetroot under cold running water and leave until cool enough to handle.

Meanwhile, gently heat the sugar and salt in the Spiced Vinegar until dissolved, stirring frequently, then bring to the boil. Take off the heat and set aside to cool.

When the beetroot are cool enough to handle, peel them and pack them into warm, clean, dry jars. Add 2 allspice berries to each jar. Pour over the vinegar, then swivel the jars to expel any air. Cover with vinegar-proof lids and seal (see pages 12-13). Store in a cool, dark, dry place for at least 1 month before eating.

Variation: if baby beetroot are not available, wrap larger beetroot in foil and bake at 180°C/350°F/gas mark 4 for 2-3 hours, depending on size. Peel and thinly slice the beetroot when they are cool, then pack them into warm, clean, dry jars. Cover with the spiced vinegar, adding 2 teaspoons salt for every 570ml/1 pint vinegar; omit the sugar.

Beetroot and Horseradish Relish

Horseradish, beetroot and apple make a fruity relish with a piquant flavour. Use a food processor rather than an ordinary grater to grate the horseradish to protect yourself against eye-watering fumes.

MAKES ABOUT 450G/1LB

450g/1lb raw beetroot
50g/2oz horseradish, grated
115g/4oz onion, chopped
225g/8oz cooking apples, such as Bramleys, peeled, cored and chopped
150g/5oz sugar
350ml/12fl oz cider vinegar

Above: Pickled Baby Beetroot are delicious eaten with cold roast meats and meat pies.

Peel the beetroot then grate coarsely into a saucepan. Add the remaining ingredients and heat gently, stirring, until the sugar has dissolved. Slowly bring to the boil and continue to boil gently for about 1¼ hours, stirring occasionally, until the vegetables and apple are tender and the relish well reduced. Ladle the relish into warm, clean, dry jars. Cover with vinegar-proof lids and seal (see pages 12-13). Store in a cool, dark, dry place for 4-6 weeks before eating

This relish will perk up cold meat pies, cold roast beef or pork, steaks and cheese.

Pickled Red Cabbage with Orange

Oranges and raisins make a fruitier, softer-flavoured pickled cabbage than normal.

MAKES ABOUT 1.8KG/4LB

1 red cabbage, weighing about 900g/2lb, halved, cored and shredded
2 tablespoons sea salt
570ml/1 pint Spiced Vinegar (see page 139), made with red wine vinegar
1 large onion, thinly sliced
50g/2oz raisins
juice and finely grated zest of 2 large oranges
1 tablespoon brown sugar

Put the cabbage into a large non-metallic bowl. Stir in the salt and leave for 8 hours.

Meanwhile, bring the Spiced Vinegar with its spices and bay leaf to the boil, then remove from the heat, cover and leave to cool.

Rinse the cabbage thoroughly, then drain and dry. Pack into warm, clean, dry jars.

Put the Spiced Vinegar, onion, raisins, orange juice, zest and sugar into a pan. Heat gently, stirring, until the sugar has dissolved, then bring to the boil. Pour over the cabbage, shaking the jars gently to make sure it is well distributed. Cover with vinegar-proof lids and seal (see pages 12-13). Store in a cool, dark, dry place for at least 1 month before eating.

Serve with cold goose or game, especially venison and hare; oxtail stew or jellied oxtail; pork pies.

Right: Pickled Red Cabbage with Orange has a delicious fruity tang and is less harshly flavoured than most ordinary red cabbage preserves.

Angel's Hair

'Angel's hair' is a rather fanciful name for this eye-catching carrot jam.

MAKES ABOUT 450G/1LB

about 300g/10oz carrots, scraped and grated to produce 225g/8oz
225g/8oz sugar
1 large lemon
3 cardamom pods, split

Put the grated carrots and sugar into a pan.

Cut the lemon peel into thin strips, squeeze the juice from the lemon, then put both into the pan with the cardamom pods.

Heat gently, stirring, until the sugar has dissolved, then boil hard for 10 minutes until very thick. Skim with a slotted spoon.

Spoon the jam into warm, clean, dry jars. Cover and seal (see pages 12-13). The jam is now ready to eat. Store in a cool, dark, dry place for up to 1 year.

Pumpkin Preserve

This attractive orange preserve can be made in November; farm shops and country markets are often the best sources.

1 pumpkin, sliced, peeled, seeds and strings
  discarded, and diced
For each 450g/1lb prepared pumpkin flesh:
450g/1lb sugar
25g/1oz fresh ginger, grated
juice of ½ lemon

Steam the pumpkin for about 20 minutes until tender.

Stir the pumpkin, sugar, ginger and lemon juice together in a non-metallic bowl, then cover the bowl and leave in a cool place for 24 hours.

Transfer the pumpkin mixture to a large, thick-bottomed saucepan, and stir over a low heat until the sugar has dissolved, then boil hard for about 15 minutes, stirring if necessary, until it is thick and translucent.

Ladle into warm, clean, dry jars. Cover

Above: bright orange Pumpkin Preserve is ideal for making at Guy Fawkes or Thanksgiving, when there are plenty of pumpkins in the shops.

and seal (see pages 12-13). Leave to cool, then store in a cool, dark, dry place for at least 1 month before eating.

Try this in place of marmalade for breakfast, or with unsalted fresh cream cheese or fromage frais for a quick pudding.

Marrows, Turnips, Gherkins, Olives

Marrow Rum

I think this is by far the best use for marrow, and although you do have to wait a long time – at least a year – to be able to appreciate it, it is well worth the wait. Use a firm marrow that is too tough for cooking or for cutting with a knife. You also need a firm cloth bag. The yield of the recipe and quantity of sugar needed will depend upon the size and juiciness of the marrow.

MAKES ABOUT 850ML-1.1LITRES/1½-2 PINTS

1 large, firm and ripe marrow
demerara, muscovado or dark brown sugar,
** to fill marrow**

Saw a thin slice off the stalk end of the marrow and reserve. Scoop the seeds and strings out of the marrow, then completely fill the cavity in the marrow with sugar. Replace the reserved slice and stick it securely in place using ordinary adhesive tape. Put the marrow in a bag of strong cloth and then hang it in a cool, dry place for 2 weeks.

Untape the marrow and top up the sugar in the cavity, then tape the top in place again and hang up the marrow in the bag. Place a bowl underneath the marrow to catch any liquid which might start to drip. Leave the marrow for 1 month.

Line a funnel with muslin and put in a clean, dry bottle.

Remove the marrow from the bag, pierce a hole where the liquid is beginning to drip and allow the liquid to run into the funnel.

Cork the bottle lightly as the liquid will bubble as it ferments. Leave in a cool, dark, dry place for a few weeks until fermentation has stopped, then cork the bottle firmly. Store in a cool, dark, dry place for 1 year before drinking.

Pickled Turnips

This pickle has a delicate sweet sharpness and light crispness that is very appealing.

MAKES ABOUT 1.2KG/2¾LB

50g/2oz sea salt
225ml/8fl oz white wine vinegar
900g/2lb small turnips, halved
1 small uncooked beetroot, peeled and sliced
2-4 garlic cloves (optional)
a few celery leaves

Gently heat 450ml/16fl oz water with the salt, stirring. Bring to the boil, remove from the heat, add the vinegar and leave to cool.

Layer the turnips, beetroot slices, garlic, if using, and the celery leaves in a clean, dry jar. Pour over the cooled brine to completely cover. Swivel the jar to expel any air. Hold the turnips down with crumpled greaseproof paper placed at the top of the jar. Seal the jar tightly (see pages 12-13) and leave on a sunny windowsill, or in a warm place for about 2 weeks before eating.

Unopened jars will keep for 3 months, but once opened they should be refrigerated.

Dill Pickled Gherkins

You will find small cucumbers in the shops from about the end of June through to September.

MAKES ABOUT 1KG/2¼LB

1kg/2¼lb small, firm gherkins
325g/11oz sea salt
700ml/1¼ pints white wine vinegar
2 teaspoons dill seeds
100g/3½oz very small pickling onions
2 garlic cloves

Put the gherkins in a non-metallic bowl, sprinkle over the salt and leave to stand in a cool place for about 24 hours.

Drain the gherkins, rinse thoroughly, then drain and dry well on paper towels. Return to the rinsed and dried bowl.

Bring the vinegar to the boil, then simmer for 5 minutes. Pour over the gherkins, cover and leave in a cold place for 1 day. Drain off the vinegar into a pan, bring it to the boil again, then leave to cool completely.

Pack the gherkins, dill, onions and garlic into a jar. Pour over vinegar to cover, then swivel the jars to expel any air. Cover the jar with a vinegar-proof lid and seal (see pages 12-13). Store in a cool, dark, dry place for at least 2 months before using.

Serve with spicy sausages, salami or pâté and fresh crusty bread.

Spiced Green Olives

Here's a good way of livening up olives that are not of the best quality. The oil can be used for salad dressings or in cooking.

MAKES 450G/1LB

225g/8oz green olives that have been packed
** in brine, rinsed**
1 tablespoon fennel seeds, lightly crushed
4 large garlic cloves, crushed
long strip of lemon zest
4 sprigs of fresh thyme
about 175ml/6fl oz olive oil

Using a meat mallet or hammer, lightly tap the olives to split them, but leave the stones intact. Alternatively, make a cut in each olive with a knife. Dry the olives on paper towels.

Pack the olives into a clean, dry jar with the fennel, garlic, lemon zest and thyme.

Pour in enough oil to cover the olives completely, swivelling the jar to expel any air. Cover and seal (see pages 12-13). Store in a cool, dark, dry place for 2 weeks before eating, shaking the jar occasionally.

Mushrooms in Oil

MAKES ABOUT 2 LITRES/3½ PINTS

50g/2oz onion, finely chopped
½ small red pepper, cored, seeded
 and finely chopped
2 garlic cloves, crushed
about 425ml/15fl oz olive oil
425ml/15fl oz white wine vinegar
few sprigs of fresh parsley
few sprigs of thyme
1 sprig of rosemary
3 fresh bay leaves
5 coriander seeds, crushed
10 black peppercorns, crushed
900g/2lb mushrooms

Gently fry the onion, pepper and garlic in
a little of the oil in a large saucepan until
softened but not coloured. Add the vinegar,
herbs, coriander seeds, peppercorns and
400ml/14fl oz water. Bring to the boil, then
continue boiling uncovered, for 10 minutes.

Put the mushrooms in a large non-metallic
bowl and pour over the saucepan contents.
Submerge the mushrooms with a plate and
leave for 12 hours; stir occasionally. Strain
off the liquid, then tip the mushrooms, herbs
and vegetables on paper towels to dry.

Using a slotted spoon, pack the herbs and
vegetables into a clean, dry jar. Slowly pour
in enough olive oil to cover completely,
pressing down on the mushrooms to expel
air. Swivel the jar to remove any air bubbles,
then cover and seal tightly (see pages 12-
13). Store in a cool, dark, dry place for at
least 3-4 weeks before eating.

Add to chicken cooked in wine, then stir in a
little crème fraîche or cream to finish. Use
the mushroom oil for frying the chicken.

Far left and left: Mushroom Ketchup and
Mushrooms in Oil. Use open-cap or field
mushrooms, or try shiitake and oyster mushrooms.

Mushroom Ketchup

MAKES ABOUT 425ML/15FL OZ

900g/2lb mushrooms, finely chopped
¼ teaspoon ground cloves
½ teaspoon each ground mace and allspice
2 anchovy fillets, chopped
300ml/10fl oz ruby port
sea salt and plenty of freshly ground
 black pepper

Bring all the ingredients and 5 tablespoons water to a slow boil in a large saucepan. Simmer for 10 minutes, stirring occasionally, until the mixture starts to thicken.

   Pour the mixture into a warm, clean, dry jar, then cover loosely and leave to cool. Seal the jar (see pages 12-13) and store in a cool, dark, dry place for at least 10 days before using.

Savoury Red Onion *Marmelade*

Savoury *marmelades* (the name comes from the French use of the word rather than the English) have become increasingly fashionable in recent years. They take a while to cook if you start from scratch, but if you pot up a batch of this version you will have a delicious, rich, sweet *marmelade* at your fingertips.

MAKES ABOUT 900G/2LB

675g/1½lb large red onions, thinly sliced
2 tablespoons olive oil
sea salt and freshly ground black pepper
150g/5oz white sugar
225ml/8fl oz red wine
4 tablespoons sherry vinegar
2 tablespoons Crème de Cassis (see page 87)
¼ teaspoon ground allspice

Cook the onions in the oil in a large frying pan or a saucepan over very low heat until they are soft. Sprinkle with salt and pepper and sugar, cover and cook for 10 minutes, stirring occasionally.

   Stir in the wine, sherry vinegar, Crème de Cassis and allspice, then raise the heat and simmer, stirring frequently, for about 30 minutes until thick.

   Ladle into warm, clean, dry jars. Cover with vinegar-proof lids and seal (see pages 12-13). Store in a cool, dark, dry place for 2 or 3 days before eating.

Serve hot or cold with grilled meats or poultry, home-made sausages, game terrine or *pâté en croûte*; serve cold with a large wedge of mature farmhouse Cheddar cheese, crusty bread and unsalted butter.

Left (clockwise from top left): shiitake, yellow oyster, oyster and chanterelle mushrooms.

Shallot *Confiture*

This *confiture* is made over a number of days to give the shallots a silky character and coax out their sweetness.

MAKES ABOUT 1.2KG/2½LB

675g/1½lb shallots, peeled, root ends intact
100g/3½oz sea salt
1 litre/1¾ pints cider vinegar
450g/1lb sugar
1½ teaspoons cloves
2 cardamom pods, crushed
1½ teaspoons caraway seeds
1 long strip of lemon zest
1 cinnamon stick
2-4 dried red chillies, crushed
good pinch of ground chilli

Put the shallots in a non-metallic bowl, sprinkle over the salt and add enough water to cover, stirring carefully to dissolve the salt. Put a plate on the shallots to submerge them, then leave for 1 day in a cool place.

   Drain and rinse the shallots thoroughly and dry on paper towels. Pour the vinegar into a pan and stir in the sugar. Place the spices, except the ground chilli, on a square of muslin and tie into a bag. Add to the pan with the ground chilli and heat gently, stirring until the sugar has dissolved. Raise the heat and boil fairly hard for 10 minutes. Remove the surface scum with a slotted spoon.

   Add the shallots and simmer very gently for 15 minutes. Remove the pan from the heat, cover and leave overnight.

   The next day, slowly bring the shallots to the boil, then simmer gently for another 15 minutes. Remove from the heat, cover and leave overnight. The next day, slowly bring the shallots to the boil once more, then simmer gently until they are golden brown and translucent. Pack into warm, clean, dry jars, taking care not to trap any air pockets. Cover with vinegar-proof lids and seal (see pages 12-13). Store in a cool, dark, dry place for at least 2 months before eating.

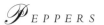
Pickled Red Peppers

Although it may seem that all red peppers are alike, there are a number of varieties available. You can also include some yellow peppers in this recipe, but I don't think green peppers work as well. Whichever you use, choose plump, fleshy ones.

MAKES 1.1 LITRES/2 PINTS

4 large, fleshy peppers, cored, seeded and cut into strips
1 small red onion, finely chopped
sea salt
25g/1oz sun-dried tomatoes
about 3 small bay leaves
about 350ml/12fl oz white wine vinegar

Layer the peppers and onion alternately in a non-metallic bowl, sprinkling each layer generously with salt. Cover with a plate to press the vegetables lightly and leave in a cool place for 24 hours, stirring gently from time to time.

Place the sun-dried tomatoes in a heat-proof bowl, pour boiling water over them and leave to soak for 5 minutes. Drain, dry on paper towels, then cut into thin strips.

Rinse the peppers and onion under cold running water, drain and dry thoroughly on paper towels. Mix the peppers, onion and tomatoes in a bowl, then pack into a clean, dry jar, adding the bay leaves. Pour in the vinegar to cover, swivelling the jar to expel any air. Cover with a vinegar-proof lid and seal (see pages 12-13). Store in a cool, dark, dry place for 2 months before eating.

———— ⌒ ————

Drain well and serve as a light starter sprinkled with virgin olive oil. Add some black olives, preferably oil-cured, strips of anchovy and a sprinkling of parsley and serve as a simple first course or part of an antipasti spread. The peppers also go well with grilled chicken and fish.

Red Pepper Relish

This richly flavoured relish goes well with hot, simply cooked meat and poultry, as well as with cold meats.

MAKES ABOUT 675G/1½LB

2 plump red peppers, cored, seeded and chopped
2 plump yellow peppers, cored, seeded and chopped
1 large onion, chopped
3 plump garlic cloves, thinly sliced
2 red chillies, seeded and chopped
2 tablespoons paprika
2 tablespoons hoisin sauce
4 tablespoons lime juice
2 tablespoons soft brown sugar
4 tablespoons mild olive oil
large pinch of sea salt

Gently heat all the ingredients together in a covered saucepan, stirring, until the sugar has dissolved, then simmer for 12-15 minutes, stirring frequently, until the vegetables are soft.

Ladle the relish into warm, clean, dry jars. Cover with vinegar-proof lids and seal (see pages 12-13). Store in a cool, dark, dry place for at least 6 weeks before eating.

Removing the skins from grilled peppers: the charred and blistered skins of grilled red peppers should be easy to peel off once cooled.

Grilled Red Peppers in Oil

Grilling adds depth to the flavour of red peppers and gives them a delicious smoky taste. Choose peppers that feel heavy for their size as they will be fleshy. The herbs can easily be adaped according to taste.

MAKES 1.4-1.7 LITRES/2½-3 PINTS

6-8 fleshy red peppers, halved lengthways
about 570-700ml/1-1¼pint white wine vinegar
2 fresh bay leaves, torn across the middle, or some small basil sprigs
about 300ml/10fl oz olive oil

Grill the red peppers under a hot grill until the skins are charred and blistered. Leave until cool enough to handle, then discard the cores and seeds and peel off the skins.

Pour the vinegar into a large saucepan and bring to the boil. Place the peppers in the boiling vinegar, cover, return quickly to the boil and boil for 45-60 seconds. Remove with a slotted spoon and spread out to dry on paper towels.

Pack the peppers into a clean jar, inserting the herbs and covering with oil as you go. Cover completely with oil and swivel the jar to expel all the air. Cover and seal (see pages 12-13). Store in a cool, dark, dry place for at least 2-3 weeks before eating.

Variation: *Stuffed Red Peppers*
Slice the grilled and blanched peppers into six pieces. Place an anchovy fillet on the inside of each piece, then roll up securely. Pack the rolls into the jar, laying a basil leaf and sliver of garlic on each layer and covering with olive oil as you go. Fill the jar, cover and seal as above.

———— ⌒ ————

Serve as antipasti, with cheese, cold meats and cold meat pies; chop and add to salads; or slice and toss with pasta (see page 33).

Fettucine with Smoked Trout, Basil and Grilled Red Peppers

Some of the best of the Mediterranean preserves can be used as the basis for effortless and delicious supper dishes. This recipe can be rustled up in the time it takes to cook some pasta.

SERVES 4

3 tablespoons oil from Grilled Red Peppers in Oil (see page 32)
3-4 spring onions finely chopped
1 garlic clove, chopped
350g/12oz fresh or dried fettucine
6 Grilled Red Peppers in Oil halves, sliced
225g/8oz smoked trout, flaked
leaves from a small handful of basil, shredded
salt and freshly ground black pepper

Gently heat the oil in a saucepan, add the spring onions and garlic and cook gently until softened but not coloured.

Meanwhile, put the fettucine in a pan of boiling salted water and cook until tender. While the pasta is cooking, add the pepper strips to the onions and garlic and heat for 1 minute, stirring, then add the trout and basil. Continue heating for a further minute, then remove from the heat and season with freshly ground black pepper.

As soon as the pasta is tender, drain and toss lightly with the red pepper mixture. Serve immediately.

Left: Fettucine with Smoked Trout, Basil and Grilled Red Peppers with (behind) Grilled Red Peppers in Oil and Middle Eastern Stuffed Aubergines in Oil.

Dried Tomatoes in Oil

If you grow your own tomatoes, or have access to a good supply, it is worth oven-drying them; they will have a good concentrated flavour. Of course, the fleshier and fuller-flavoured the tomatoes, the better the end result.

2kg/4½lb fleshy, ripe tomatoes
sea salt
bunch of fresh herbs such as basil, or thyme and
  marjoram with a little rosemary (optional)
1 bay leaf or 2-3 sprigs of dried oregano
  (optional)
4-5 garlic cloves (optional)
virgin olive oil

Preheat the oven to its lowest setting. Line the bottom of the oven with foil to protect it from the drips from the tomatoes.

Halve the tomatoes lengthways and scoop out the seeds using a teaspoon. As each tomato half is ready, place it cut-side down on a few thicknesses of paper towels.

Sprinkle salt very lightly on to each tomato half then place them, cut-side down, on a wire rack, spacing them slightly apart.

Put the racks in the oven and prop the door very slightly ajar with a skewer (or something similar) so that the tomatoes dry out rather than cook. Leave for 6-12 hours depending on the size of the tomatoes and the temperature of the oven, until the tomatoes feel dry but are still slightly fleshy (they should not become papery). Remove from the oven and leave to cool.

Loosely pack the tomatoes in clean, dry jars, adding the herbs and garlic, if using. Pour in olive oil to cover and swivel the jars to expel any air. Cover and seal the jar (see pages 12-13). Store in a cool, dark, dry place for at least 2-4 weeks before eating.

Right: Dried Tomatoes in Oil are a visually striking focus for these delicious Polenta Rolls.

Dried Tomato and Polenta Rolls

MAKES 6-12 ROLLS

300g/10oz strong flour, plus extra for kneading
1 teaspoon salt
175g/6oz polenta
1 teaspoon dried oregano or *herbes de Provence*
1 sachet easy-blend yeast
2 tablespoons oil from Dried Tomatoes in Oil,
  plus extra for brushing (see left)
50g/2oz Dried Tomatoes in Oil, drained
  and chopped
sea salt

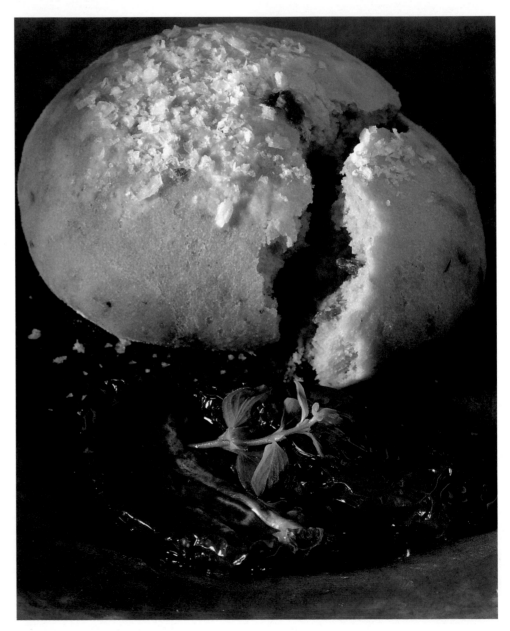

34

 *T*OMATOES

Sift the flour and salt into a bowl, then stir in the polenta, herbs and yeast. Make a well in the centre and slowly pour in 250ml/9fl oz water and the oil, stirring together to make a smooth, sticky dough that is too wet to knead. Cover and leave in a draught-free place until doubled in volume and frothy.

Knock back the dough and turn it on to a floured surface. Knead for about 15 minutes, working in as much flour as needed to make a soft dough. Flatten the dough, sprinkle the tomatoes on top and continue to knead for about 5 minutes, by which time the tomatoes should be evenly distributed.

Lightly flour a baking sheet. Form the dough into 6-12 rolls, place on the baking sheet and leave to rise in a draught-free place until doubled in volume. Preheat the oven to 220°C/425°F/gas mark 7.

Brush the rolls with a little extra oil and sprinkle with sea salt. Bake the rolls for 12-20 minutes depending on size, until they are risen, lightly browned and the undersides sound hollow when tapped.

Green Tomato Chutney

Almost everybody who grows tomatoes seems to end up with some green ones. The best way to use these up is to make chutney. The quantity of garlic may seem excessive, but the flavour mellows during cooking and storage.

MAKES ABOUT 675G/1½LB

1kg/2¼lb green tomatoes, coarsely chopped
115g/4oz fresh ginger, thinly sliced
3 fresh green chillies, seeded and chopped
23 large garlic cloves, chopped
1 tablespoon brown sugar
1 teaspoon sea salt
570ml/1 pint cider vinegar

Put all the ingredients except for the vinegar in a saucepan, then add half the vinegar and

bring to the boil. Simmer, stirring frequently, for about 20 minutes until the ingredients are tender. Add the remaining vinegar.

Bring to the boil again, then simmer until the chutney is well reduced and there is no free liquid.

Ladle the chutney into warm, clean, dry jars. Cover with vinegar-proof lids and seal (see pages 12-13). Store in a cool, dark, dry place for 1 month before eating.

Tomato Ketchup

MAKES ABOUT 1.1 LITRES/2 PINTS

2.2kg/5lb ripe tomatoes, chopped
1½ fleshy red peppers, cored, seeded and chopped
2 large red onions, chopped
4 garlic cloves, chopped
225ml/8fl oz red wine vinegar
1 teaspoon celery or mustard seeds
1 small piece of mace blade
1 teaspoon black peppercorns
¾-1 teaspoon paprika pepper
pinch of cayenne pepper
1 teaspoon rock or sea salt
1 tablespoon tarragon vinegar (optional)

Gently cook the tomatoes, peppers, onions and garlic in 115ml/4fl oz of the red wine vinegar until very soft, then increase the heat and boil rapidly, stirring frequently, until the liquid evaporates and the mixture becomes very thick.

Use a wooden spoon to press the vegetables through a non-metallic sieve. Discard the juice, then return the vegetables to the pan. Tie the celery or mustard seeds, mace and peppercorns in a square of muslin and add to the pan with the paprika, cayenne, salt, remaining red wine vinegar and tarragon vinegar, if using. Bring to the boil then simmer, stirring frequently, until very thick. Remove from the heat and take out the muslin bag.

Pour into warm, clean, dry bottles. Cover with vinegar-proof lids and seal (see pages 12-13). Process in a boiling waterbath for 30 minutes (see pages 12-13). Store in a cool, dark, dry place for at least 2 weeks before eating and 9-12 months in total.

Tomato and Red Pepper Relish

There is relatively little vinegar in this recipe, which makes it a very mild relish. The addition of a little chilli makes it more lively. If you are unable to keep the heat sufficiently low on a gas hob use a heat diffusing mat.

MAKES ABOUT 1.5KG/2¾LB

4 tablespoons olive oil
225g/8oz Spanish onion, finely chopped
2 large, fleshy red peppers, cored, seeded and chopped
1 garlic clove, crushed
1 fresh red chilli, seeded and finely chopped (optional)
½ teaspoon each of ground allspice, ground ginger, paprika and salt
450g/1lb ripe tomatoes, peeled and chopped
225g/8oz sugar
150ml/5fl oz white wine vinegar

Heat the oil in a saucepan, then add the onion and cook gently until very soft. Add the peppers, garlic, chilli if using, spices and salt and cook for 10 minutes.

Stir in the remaining ingredients, cover and cook very slowly for at least 1¼ hours until the relish is thickened but not too thick. Stir occasionally for most of the time but more frequently towards the end to prevent the relish from sticking.

Ladle the relish into warm, clean, dry jars. Cover with vinegar-proof lids and seal (see pages 12-13). Store in a cool, dark, dry place for 2 months before eating.

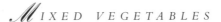

Ratatouille Chutney

This is my chosen proportion of vegetables but, with the exception of tomatoes, they can be altered according to taste.

MAKES ABOUT 1.8KG/4LB

1kg/2¼lb tomatoes, peeled and finely chopped
350g/12oz onions, finely chopped
350g/12oz aubergines, finely diced
350g/12oz courgettes, finely diced
350g/12oz red peppers, cored, seeded
 and finely diced
225g/8oz green peppers, cored, seeded
 and finely diced
3 garlic cloves, crushed
1 tablespoon paprika
1 tablespoon cayenne pepper
1¼ tablespoon coriander seeds
1 tablespoon sea salt
350g/12oz sugar
300ml/10fl oz red wine vinegar

Toast the coriander seeds in a heavy-based, preferably non-stick, frying pan for ½-1 minute over a low heat, stirring to prevent them from burning, until they are fragrant. Remove the seeds from the pan and crush them lightly with a pestle or the end of a rolling-pin. Set aside.

Gently heat the vegetables, garlic, spices and salt together in a covered saucepan for about 10 minutes, stirring occasionally, until the juices run. Uncover and bring to the boil, then simmer for 1 hour until the vegetables are soft and most of the liquid has evaporated off.

Over a low heat, stir in the sugar and vinegar until the sugar has dissolved, then simmer for another hour, stirring occasionally, until the chutney is very thick and there is no free liquid.

Ladle the chutney into warm, clean, dry jars. Cover the jars with vinegar-proof lids and seal (see pages 12-13). Store the chutney in a cool, dark, dry place for at least 1 month before eating.

Italian Garden Pickle

As the name suggests, this pickle uses all the vegetables that would be found in an Italian country garden. It makes a very colourful and delicious preserve.

MAKES 1.7 LITRES/3 PINTS

225g/8oz red onions
1 red pepper, cored, seeded and cut into chunks
1 aubergine, cut into thick matchsticks
225g/8oz small courgettes, cut into thick
 matchsticks
1 small fennel bulb, cut into wedges
115g/4oz button mushrooms
175g/6oz sea salt
115g/4oz cherry tomatoes
4-6 garlic cloves, sliced
7 tablespoons walnut oil
700ml/1¼ pints white wine vinegar
2-3 small sprigs fresh bay leaves or rosemary
several sprigs tarragon
2 teaspoons black peppercorns, lightly crushed

Trim the red onions, leaving the root end intact, then cut lengthways into thick wedges. Layer all the vegetables, except the tomatoes and the garlic, in a non-metallic bowl, sprinkling salt between the layers. Pour over 1.7 litres/3 pints water, use a plate to keep the vegetables submerged and leave in a cool place overnight.

Drain the vegetables and rinse them well, then leave them to dry thoroughly spread out on paper towels.

Tip the vegetables into a bowl and stir in the tomatoes, garlic, and walnut oil. Pour a thin layer of vinegar into the bottom of a large, clean, dry jar and add a bay leaf or rosemary sprig and a tarragon sprig.

Using a spoon, pack the vegetables into the jar, adding peppercorns and the remaining herbs as you go so they are evenly distributed. Pour vinegar over each layer. Cover the vegetables completely with vinegar, swivel the jar to expel all the air, then cover with a vinegar-proof lid and seal

(see pages 12-13). Store in a cool, dark, dry place for at least 1 month before eating.

───⌣───

Serve lightly dressed with oil as part of an antipasto, or with cold meats, pies and cheeses.

Indonesian Cauliflower Pickle

This is a nutty, spicy vegetable pickle.

MAKES ABOUT 675G/1½LB

2 plump garlic cloves, crushed
25g/1oz piece of fresh ginger, peeled
 and grated
2 teaspoons ground turmeric
3 tablespoons groundnut oil
150ml/5fl oz Spiced Vinegar (see page 139)
175g/6oz cauliflower florets
1 large red pepper, cored, seeded and chopped
½ cucumber, sliced
1-2 green chillies, seeded
4 tablespoons sesame seeds
115g/4oz dark or light soft brown sugar
115g/4oz salted peanuts, chopped

In a saucepan, gently heat the garlic, ginger and turmeric in the oil for about 5 minutes, stirring occasionally, until fragrant. Stir in the vinegar.

Bring to the boil, then add the cauliflower, pepper and cucumber and return to the boil. Cover and simmer until the vegetables are tender. Stir in the remaining ingredients.

Ladle the chutney into warm, clean, dry jars. Swivel the jars to expel any air. Cover with vinegar-proof lids and seal (see pages 12-13). Store in a cool, dark, dry place for 2 months before eating.

───⌣───

This pickle goes well with hard cheeses.

Pickled Vegetables with Ginger and Mint

Ginger, mint and rice vinegar produce deliciously delicate pickled vegetables. Rice vinegar is available from specialist food shops and some supermarkets. It is mild so it does not have the same preserving properties of other vinegars; you should, therefore, use the pickle within 6 months.

MAKES 1.1 LITRES/2 PINTS

1kg/2¼lb mixed vegetables, such as small
  fennel bulbs, small carrots, celery sticks, red
  and yellow peppers, plump spring onions
  and cauliflower
115g/4oz sea salt
several sprigs of fresh mint
8g/¼oz piece of plump, fresh ginger,
  peeled and thinly sliced
800ml/28fl oz rice vinegar

Prepare the vegetables: cut the fennel into slim wedges; quarter the carrots and celery sticks; core, seed and slice the peppers; remove most of the green part from the spring onions; divide the cauliflower into small florets.

Layer the vegetables with the salt in a large non-metallic bowl. Cover with a lightly weighted plate to press the vegetables slightly and leave for 8-12 hours.

Rinse the vegetables under cold running water, drain well and dry thoroughly on kitchen paper. Pack into clean, dry jars, adding mint and ginger at regular intervals.

Pour in vinegar to cover the vegetables and swivel the jars to expel any air bubbles, then cover with vinegar-proof lids and seal (see pages 12-13). Store in a cool, dark, dry place for at least 1 month before using.

Left: Pickled Vegetables with Ginger and Mint is made using rice vinegar for a preserve that is deliciously delicate.

HOT, SPICY AND SALTY

Preserves made from hot, spicy or salty ingredients come from all around the world. The preserves in this chapter will really add a 'lift' and give a flavour boost to the dishes you serve them with. They range from a fiery Red Curry Paste (see page 40) from Thailand, to Japanese Pickled Ginger (see page 48) and Harissa (see page 42), a great staple of Tunisian cooking. You can increase or decrease the quantity of chillies you use in each recipe depending on whether you like fiery food or just a hint of heat. As they are generally used in small quantities; the preserves on the following pages will add a touch of spice to countless mealtimes.

Left (from left to right): Chinese-style Shallots, Pickled Mixed Chillies and Pickled Eggs.

Harvey's Sauce

This is a classic British sauce that ranks alongside Worcestershire sauce in versatility.

MAKES 570ML/1 PINT

**1 head of garlic, divided into cloves
 and chopped
1 shallot, chopped
6 anchovy fillets, drained and chopped
570ml/1 pint red wine vinegar
1 tablespoon cayenne pepper**

Stir all the ingredients together in a non-metallic bowl, cover and leave in a cool place for 2 weeks, stirring 2 or 3 times a day to disperse the flavours.

Strain through a non-metallic sieve lined with a double thickness of muslin, then pour into bottles. Cover with vinegar-proof lids (see pages 12-13). Store in a cool, dark, dry place for 1 month before using.

Enhances the flavour of bland fish, fish soups or casseroles; can be used in sauces for fish and white or cheese sauces.

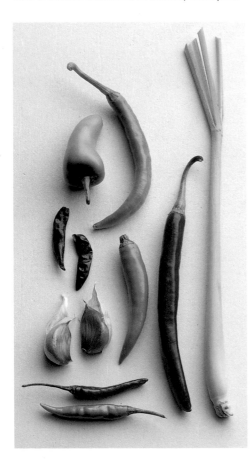

Left (clockwise from top left): Jalapeño, cayenne pepper, lime grass, tabasco chilli, orange chilli, red and green chillies, garlic, Serrano chillies.

Mediterranean Spread

Use French wholegrain mustard as it is usually more piquant than English brands.

MAKES ABOUT 225G/8OZ

**50g/2oz can anchovy fillets in oil
50g/2oz Dried Tomatoes in Oil (see page 34),
 drained
25g/1oz capers, preferably packed in salt
200g/7oz pitted oil-cured black olives, drained
2 garlic cloves, whole
1 teaspoon French wholegrain mustard
pinch of ground allspice
1 teaspoon brandy
about 5 tablespoons olive oil, plus extra
 for covering
freshly ground black pepper**

Put the anchovy fillets and their oil, the dried tomatoes, capers, olives, garlic, mustard and allspice in a food processor or blender and process to make a fairly smooth paste. Briefly mix in the brandy then, with the motor running, slowly pour in the olive oil. Add pepper to taste.

Spoon the spread into a clean, dry jar, spoon a little olive oil on the top and cover tightly. Store in a cool, dark, dry place for at least 2 days before using. This will keep in the refrigerator, covered, for 6-8 weeks.

Spread on fresh, crusty bread, then top with a cool soft cheese such as goats' cheese; use a little to top grilled beef, lamb or pork steaks and chops, or grilled aubergine slices; insert under the skin of chicken before grilling or roasting; mash with the yolks of hard-boiled eggs and spoon back into the whites for delicious stuffed eggs.

Red Curry Paste

This is a typical Thai red curry paste but, conveniently, all the ingredients can be bought from most supermarkets.

MAKES ABOUT 65ML/4 TABLESPOONS

**1 teaspoon cumin seeds
1 tablespoon coriander seeds
1 teaspoon black peppercorns
4 garlic cloves, chopped
2.5cm/1in piece of fresh root ginger, peeled
 and finely chopped
1 teaspoon finely grated lime zest
2 stalks lemon grass, bulbs only, finely chopped
about 8 dried red chillies, seeded if liked (to
 reduce the heat), chopped
2 teaspoons shrimp paste**

Heat a heavy-based, preferably non-stick, frying pan over a low heat then add the cumin and coriander seeds and heat for ½-1 minutes until fragrant. Tip into a mortar or small blender and crush lightly. Add the remaining ingredients and pound or mix to a paste.

Spoon the mixture into a clean, dry jar. Cover and store in a cool, dark, dry place for at least 2 days before using, then keep in the refrigerator for 6-8 weeks.

Use to add zest to casseroles and sauces; spread sparingly on meats before grilling, or on bread for savoury sandwiches.

Thai Prawn Curry

Unlike Indian curries which need long, slow simmering, Thai curries need very little cooking time. The fish sauce and coconut milk can be found in most good supermarkets and specialist or ethnic food shops.

SERVES 2-3

2 tablespoons groundnut oil
1 plump garlic clove, finely chopped
1 tablespoon Red Curry Paste (see page 40)
225ml/8fl oz coconut milk
2 tablespoons fish sauce
1 teaspoon sugar (optional)
12 raw large prawns, about 7.5cm/3in long,
 shells and heads removed but tails left intact
zest of 2-3 limes, finely grated
10 basil leaves, torn

Heat the oil in a frying pan over a medium heat, then add the garlic and cook until pale gold and fragrant. Stir in the Red Curry Paste and heat briefly, then stir in half the coconut milk, the fish sauce and the sugar, if using.

Add the prawns and cook, turning once, for 2-3 minutes until they begin to turn opaque. Add the remaining coconut milk and the lime zest and continue cooking until the prawns are cooked through. Add the torn basil leaves and serve with plain boiled or basmati rice.

Left: the flavours of plump prawns, coconut milk, fresh basil and Red Curry Paste mingle in this fragrant Thai Prawn Curry.

Harissa

Harissa, or 'arhissa' as this is sometimes called, is a fiery paste made from chillies. It is primarily associated with Tunisian cooking, but it is also used in Algerian and Moroccan cuisine. It is served as a condiment, in a small dish with a small spoon, and used in cooking and as an accompaniment to couscous.

MAKES 75ML/5 TABLESPOONS

25g/1oz dried red chillies
1 garlic clove, chopped
1 teaspoon coriander seeds
1 teaspoon cumin seeds
1 teaspoon caraway seeds
pinch of sea salt
3 tablespoons olive oil

Put the chillies in a bowl, cover with hot water and leave to soak for 1 hour.

Drain the chillies and put them in a mortar, spice grinder or small blender with the garlic, coriander, cumin and caraway seeds and salt. Mix to a paste, then stir in 2 tablespoons olive oil.

Transfer to a small jar and pour a little oil over the surface. Cover and store in a cool, dark, dry place for 1 day before using. This lasts for about 4 months.

Harissa is a versatile seasoning that will add 'life' to many savoury dishes; add it to meat, poultry or vegetable casseroles, saffron-flavoured fish soups and stews, 'stewed' red peppers and tomatoes used as a base for poached eggs, or add to salad dressings.

Mix a little Harissa with peeled, seeded and finely chopped well-flavoured tomatoes, add a pinch of salt and serve as a dipping sauce for kebabs.

Right: Fresh 'Hot' Tomato and Red Pepper Relish is quickly made from home-made store-cupboard preserves and brings any meal to life.

Fresh 'Hot' Tomato and Red Pepper Relish

When you want to add a little 'heat' to dishes, simply dip a small spoon into a pot of Harissa instead of seeding and chopping chillies. For this vibrant relish, you can make use of another recipe in this book, Grilled Red Peppers in Oil (page 32). If you do not have any to hand, grill a fresh red pepper until charred and blistered, then peel it (see page 32). When you drain off the oil, save it for making salad dressings.

SERVES 4

500g/18oz well-flavoured tomatoes
1-2 garlic cloves, unpeeled
2 halves Grilled Red Peppers in Oil
 (see page 32), chopped
1-2 teaspoons Harissa (see left)
sea salt
2 tablespoons oil from the Peppers or
 2 tablespoons virgin olive oil

Preheat the grill to medium high.

Grill the tomatoes and garlic cloves, turning them occasionally, until charred and blistered; the garlic should be soft. Leave until cool enough to handle, then peel, seed and coarsely chop the tomatoes; peel and chop the garlic.

Mix together the tomatoes, garlic, peppers, Harissa, salt to taste and oil. Set aside for 2 hours.

Drain off the oil and spoon into a clean, dry jar. Cover tightly, then store in a cool, dark, dry place for 1 month before use.

Serve with grilled or fried meats or poultry; baked, poached, grilled or fried fish; on bread or as part of a salad.

Tomatillo and Chilli Relish

Tomatillos are sometimes called Mexican green tomatoes but they are not related to tomatoes. In fact, tomatillos are a relative of the Cape gooseberry and, although green and acidic when unripe (like most fruits), when ripe and bright yellow, they have a papery outer covering similar to the Cape gooseberry. The flavour is slightly reminiscent of apple, and it develops on cooking. Modify the heat of this relish by adjusting the number of chillies and removing the chilli seeds for a milder flavour.

MAKES ABOUT 200G/7OZ

8 fresh tomatillos, loose skins removed
10 fresh green chillies
3 garlic cloves
1 onion, quartered
75g/3oz sugar
5 tablespoons cider vinegar
1 teaspoon ground cinnamon
1 teaspoon sea salt

Mix all the ingredients in a blender or food processor to the texture you require. Pour into a pan and simmer, stirring frequently, for about 20 minutes until the relish is thick.

Pour into a warm, clean, dry jar, loosely cover with a vinegar-proof lid and process in a waterbath for 20 minutes (see page 13). Store in a cool, dark, dry place for 1 month before using. Once opened, refrigerate. If not processed in a waterbath, it will keep for 1 month in total in the refrigerator.

Serve with Mexican-style dishes or with meat or poultry.

Pickled Mixed Chillies

A mixture of colours, varieties and sizes gives added interest to the look and flavour of this recipe, but it is still worth making if you can only find chillies that are all more or less the same.

MAKES 1-1.1 LITRES/1¾-2 PINTS

225g/8oz mixed fresh chillies, whole
1 small dried red chilli, crushed
3 garlic cloves
1 teaspoon coriander seeds, lightly crushed
1 teaspoon cloves
2 bay leaves
570ml/1 pint white wine vinegar, warmed
2 teaspoons caster sugar

Place the whole, fresh chillies in a saucepan, cover with water and bring to a simmer. Continue simmering for 5 minutes.

Using a slotted spoon, transfer the chillies to paper towels to dry, then pack them into a clean, dry jar. Add the remaining ingredients and swivel the jar to dissolve the sugar and to expel any air. Cover with a vinegar-proof lid and seal (see pages 12-13). Store in a cool, dark, dry place for 2 weeks, shaking the jar occasionally, before eating.

Hot Pepper Sauce

The exact degree of 'heat' in this colourful curry-flavoured sauce will be determined by the type of chillies you use (small ones are generally hotter than large ones), whether the seeds are left in or removed and, of course, the number used. Additionally, the amount of mustard powder used influences the fieriness.

MAKES 850ML/1½ PINTS

1 small green mango
2 onions, finely chopped
2 garlic cloves, finely chopped
about 10-12 fresh red chillies, seeded, if liked, and chopped
1 teaspoon curry powder
½ teaspoon turmeric
2 teaspoons table salt
425ml/15fl oz white wine vinegar
4 tablespoons English mustard powder

Put the whole mango in a saucepan and just cover with water, then bring to the boil. Cover and simmer for about 10 minutes. Drain and leave the mango until cool enough to handle, then peel and coarsely chop.

Put the mango, onions, garlic, chillies, curry, turmeric, salt and 400ml/14fl oz of the vinegar in a saucepan and simmer gently for 15 minutes, stirring occasionally.

In a small bowl, stir the remaining vinegar into the mustard, then stir the mixture into the pan and bring to the boil. Remove from the heat and pour into a warm, clean, dry jar. Cover with a vinegar-proof lid and seal (see pages 12-13). Store in a cool, dark, dry place for 1 month before eating.

Use in casseroles, marinades and salad dressings; and as a relish.

*M*USTARDS

Tarragon Mustard

Unlike making mustard from English mustard powder, which is ready to eat after being left to stand for a short while, this mustard should be kept for at least 2 weeks to allow the flavours to mature.

MAKES ABOUT 150G/6OZ

25g/1oz yellow mustard seeds
75g/3oz black mustard seeds
100ml/3½fl oz dry white wine
1 tablespoon white wine vinegar
leaves from a small bunch of fresh tarragon,
 finely chopped
1 tablespoon sea salt

Grind the mustard seeds in a spice grinder or small blender as finely as you like – the finer the grind the hotter the mustard. Tip them into a non-metallic bowl, then stir in 3 tablespoons water and leave for 10 minutes before adding the remaining ingredients. Stir together well.

   Transfer the mustard to clean, dry pots. Cover loosely with vinegar-proof lids and leave to stand overnight at room temperature. The next day, stir, then cover tightly and store in a cool, dark, dry place for at least 2 weeks before eating.

Mustard Dipping Sauce

This sauce is thinner than the Sweet Mustard Sauce which follows this recipe.

MAKES ABOUT 210ML/7½FL OZ

6 tablespoons soy sauce
3 tablespoons Dijon mustard
6 tablespoons saké
several drops of Tabasco sauce

In a small bowl, whisk the soy sauce into the mustard then whisk in the saké. Add Tabasco sauce to taste and whisk together.

Grain Mustard

The mustard seeds needed for this recipe are sold in Indian, Chinese or health food shops; do not use seeds sold for sowing.

MAKES ABOUT 230ML/8FL OZ

50g/2oz black mustard seeds
25g/1oz yellow mustard seeds
115ml/4fl oz white wine vinegar
1 shallot, finely chopped
1 tablespoon sea salt

Above: Grain Mustard is particularly delicious eaten with cold ham and fresh bread.

Soak the mustard seeds in the vinegar in a non-metallic bowl for 24 hours.

   Stir in the salt and crush the seeds to a coarse paste using a pestle or the end of a rolling pin, adding a little more vinegar if necessary. Transfer to clean, dry jars, cover tightly with vinegar-proof lids and seal. Store in a cool, dark, dry place for at least 2 weeks before using.

Mustard, Eggs, Onions

Pour the sauce into a clean, dry bottle, then cover and seal. The sauce can be used immediately but is best left for up to 4 hours. Shake well before using. Store in a cool, dark, dry place for up to 1 year.

Sweet Mustard Sauce

Mirin, Japanese sweetened saké, adds a touch of sweetness to this versatile sauce. You can buy mirin from good supermarkets or speciality food shops.

MAKES ABOUT 250ML/9FL OZ

3 tablespoons rice wine vinegar
6 tablespoons Dijon mustard
6 tablespoons mild oil, such as mild olive
 or sunflower oil
3 tablespoons mirin

In a small bowl, whisk the vinegar into the mustard then slowly pour in the oil, still whisking (see below). Add the mirin and whisk together.

 Pour into a clean, dry bottle, cover and seal (see pages 12-13). Leave for 2-4 hours and shake before using. This will keep in a cool, dark, dry place for at least 6 months.

Adding the oil: pour the oil into the vinegar and mustard mixture in a slow, steady stream, whisking constantly.

Pickled Eggs

These are easy to prepare and versatile. It used to be customary to dip the eggs into salt before each bite. As the eggs are used, they can be replaced with freshly cooked ones, but try to ease these to the bottom of the jar so all the eggs are eaten in rotation.

MAKES 1.8KG/4LB

850ml/1½ pints cider vinegar or
 white wine vinegar
2.5cm/1in piece fresh ginger
1 tablespoon coriander seeds
2 dried red chillies
2 garlic cloves, crushed (optional)
1½ tablespoons black peppercorns
12 hard-boiled eggs, peeled

Put all the ingredients, except the eggs, in a large saucepan and bring to the boil, then simmer for about 10 minutes. Remove from the heat, cover and leave to cool.

 Pack the eggs into clean, dry jars then strain in the vinegar through a non-metallic sieve to cover the eggs completely. Cover with vinegar-proof lids and seal (see pages 12-13). Store in a cool, dark, dry place for 6-8 weeks before eating or up to 1 year.

Chinese-style Shallots

These shallots provide an interesting alternative to pickled onions. Small onions and garlic can be preserved too.

MAKES 1.4KG/3LB

1.4kg/3lb shallots
1 dried red chilli
3 slices fresh ginger
about 570ml/1 pint soy sauce,
 preferably shoyu

Place the shallots in a heat-proof bowl, pour boiling water over and leave for 2 minutes.

 Drain the shallots, then trim and peel them. Pack into a clean, dry 1.4kg/3lb jar with the chilli and ginger. Pour in soy sauce to cover completely. Cover and seal the jar (see pages 12-13). Store in a cool, dark, dry place for 4-6 months before eating.

Indian Pickled Onions

The red wine vinegar in this recipe turns the onions pink. To make peeling the onions easier, cut off the root and tip ends, pour boiling water over them, and leave them for a minute or so, then drain and rinse quickly under running cold water. Use a stainless steel knife to prevent discoloration.

MAKES ABOUT 1.1 LITRES/2 PINTS

450g/1lb pickling onions
50g/2oz sea salt
450ml/16fl oz red wine vinegar
2 garlic cloves, sliced
2 dried red chillies

Cut a deep cross from the top to the bottom of each onion but leave them attached at the base. Dissolve the salt in 570ml/1 pint water in a non-metallic bowl, then add the onions, cover and leave for one day at room temperature, stirring occasionally.

 Drain and rinse the onions thoroughly, then dry well on paper towels. Pack the onions into a 1.1 litre/2 pint jar. If there are a few too many onions, they may be reserved and used in cooking.

 Mix together the vinegar, garlic and chillies and pour over the onions to cover them completely; if the onions float, put crumpled greaseproof paper in the jar to keep the onions submerged. Swivel the jar to expel any air, then cover with vinegar-proof lids and seal (see pages 12-13). Store in a cool, dark, dry place for 1 month before eating.

Indian Carrot Sticks in Oil

Mustard oil is used a great deal in Bengali and Kashmiri cooking. It has a split personality, smelling fiery when cold but loosing its pungency when heated and becoming slightly sweet.

MAKES 1 LITRE/1¾ PINTS

450g/1lb carrots, cut into matchsticks
sea salt
at least 1 tablespoon black mustard seeds,
 to taste
1 teaspoon cayenne pepper
1 teaspoon ground turmeric
½-¾ pint mustard oil or groundnut oil,
 to cover, warmed if liked

Bring a large saucepan of salted water to the boil, add the carrots and continue boiling for about 5 minutes. Drain well, then spread out on paper towels to dry.

   In a small bowl, crush the mustard seeds with a pestle or the end of a rolling pin, so they split in half or into quarters. Place in a small bowl and mix together with the cayenne pepper, turmeric and about 115ml/4fl oz oil.

   Using a spoon, pack the carrots into a clean, dry jar. Pour in the flavoured oil and top up with more oil to cover the carrots completely. Swivel the jar to expel all the air bubbles. Cover and seal (see pages 12-13). Store in a cool, dark, dry place for 1 month, shaking the jar daily for the first 10 days or so, before eating. Shake the jar before serving the carrots.

Serve with aperitifs; as part of an Indian meal; or as an accompaniment to cold meats, pies, pâtés and hard cheeses.

Right: serve these Carrot Sticks with Indian-style meals or use them to perk up Western foods.

Mixed Vegetables

Creole Chow-Chow

Chinese migrant railroad workers in mid-nineteenth-century America introduced this hot pickled chow into American cuisine. It is not unlike Indian-spiced piccalilli.

MAKES ABOUT 4KG/8LB

225g/8oz white cabbage, shredded
450g/1lb whole French beans
2 red peppers, cored, seeded and diced
1 green pepper, cored, seeded and diced
450g/1lb cucumber, chopped
1 small cauliflower, broken into florets
675g/1½lb green tomatoes, chopped
225g/8oz button or pickling onions
5 tablespoons sea salt
2.3 litres/4 pints cider vinegar
50g/2oz fresh horseradish, grated
8 garlic cloves, crushed
2 tablespoons black mustard seeds
115g/4oz French mustard
15g/½oz turmeric
175g/6oz light soft brown sugar
150ml/5fl oz olive oil or sunflower oil

Layer the vegetables and salt in a large non-metallic colander and leave to drain for about 12 hours, stirring occasionally.

Place the rest of the ingredients in a large saucepan, stir together and bring to the boil. Simmer for 5 minutes, stirring constantly. Add the vegetables, without rinsing, and return to the boil. Simmer for 15-20 minutes ensuring that the vegetables remain crisp. Pack into clean, dry jars, cover and seal (see pages 12-13). Store in a cool, dark, dry place for 2 weeks before eating.

Serve with cold meats, mature cheeses and fresh, crusty bread.

Mixed Vegetable Pickle

Don't feel you have to use the selection of vegetables I have given; omit some or use substitutes according to taste.

You can use a crinkle-edged cutter to slice the vegetables and layer them by variety or by colour in the jar, to make an extremely attractive (as well as delicious) pickle.

MAKES 1.7 LITRES/3 PINTS

4 fresh or dried red chillies
2 blades of mace
1½ cinnamon sticks
8 allspice berries
2 bay leaves, torn
about 1.1 litres/2 pints white wine vinegar
sea salt
**about 250g/9oz carrots, cut into 1.25cm/
   ½in slices**
115g/4oz baby sweetcorn
**1 celeriac bulb, or 225g/8oz small turnips,
   cut into 1.25cm/½in slices**
4 celery stalks, cut into 1.25cm/½in slices
**1 large red pepper, cored, seeded, quartered
   and cut into 1.25cm/½in slices**
250g/9oz broccoli florets
**100g/3½oz mange-touts or French beans,
   topped and tailed**
150g/5oz pickling onions

Preparing red peppers: cut out and discard the core along with any seeds, before removing the white veins.

Place the chillies, mace, cinnamon, allspice berries and bay leaves in a saucepan, pour in the vinegar, bring to the boiling point, then boil for 2 minutes. Remove from the heat, cover, and leave overnight.

Add the carrots, sweetcorn, celeriac or turnips, and celery to a large saucepan of boiling salted water and boil for 10 minutes. Add the remaining vegetables and boil for 7-10 minutes until they are just tender.

Drain the vegetables and spread out to dry on paper towels. Strain the vinegar, then pour a little into a clean, dry jar. Using a spoon, pack the vegetables into the jar, adding a little vinegar. Cover the vegetables with vinegar and swivel the jar to expel any air. Cover with a vinegar-proof lid and seal (see pages 12-13). Store in a cool, dark, dry place for 1-3 months before eating.

Easy Pickle

This easy-to-make pickle is ready for eating after 24 hours and keeps for up to 1 year.

MAKES 900G/2LB

**225g/8oz baby onions, or 1 small Spanish
   onion, thinly sliced**
4 celery stalks, thinly sliced
**2 small cooking apples, preferably Bramleys,
   peeled, cored (see page 56) and thinly sliced**
115ml/4fl oz soy sauce
115ml/4fl oz medium-dry sherry
1 teaspoon chilli powder
225ml/8fl oz white wine vinegar

Pack the onions, celery and apples into a clean, dry jar. In a small bowl, stir together the soy sauce, sherry and chilli powder, then pour over the vegetables. Cover with vinegar and swivel the jar to expel any air bubbles.

Cover the jar with a vinegar-proof lid and seal (see pages 12-13), then shake it to mix in the vinegar. Store in a cool, dark, dry place for at least 24 hours before eating.

Pickled Garlic in Oil

The flavour of the garlic mellows over time. After 3 or 4 months it tastes of lightly poached garlic and still has a bit of crunch. After 6 months it can easily be crushed to add to vegetable and meat dishes, or to meat cooking juices to make a quick sauce.

MAKES ABOUT 225G/8OZ

225g/8oz garlic cloves
3 tablespoons fennel seeds
1 tablespoon black peppercorns
1 tablespoon garam masala
1 tablespoon black onion seeds (nigella)
1 teaspoon chilli powder
1 tablespoon sea salt
about 175ml/6fl oz groundnut oil

Pack the garlic cloves into a jar and add the spices and salt. Pour over enough oil to cover the garlic completely, then cover and seal the jar (see pages 12-13).

Leave in a sunny or warm place for 1 week, swivelling the jar several times a day, then leave for a further week. Transfer to normal room temperature and store in a cool, dark, dry place for at least 2 months before eating.

Japanese Pickled Ginger

Japanese pickled ginger comes in two forms: *gari,* also known as *amuzu-shoga,* which is yellowish or delicate salmon pink depending on the length of preservation; and *beni-shoga* which is dyed garish pink.

MAKES 350G/12OZ

225g/8oz piece of fresh ginger, cut into wafer-
 thin slices with a sharp knife or a mandolin
sea salt
1 tablespoon sugar
225ml/8fl oz rice vinegar
few drops of edible red food colouring (optional)

Place the ginger in a small bowl of very cold water to soak for 30 minutes.

Drain the ginger, then add it to a saucepan of boiling water. Return to the boil, then drain and leave the ginger to cool.

Put the ginger slices into a clean, dry jar, sprinkling them with a little salt.

In a saucepan, gently heat the sugar in the vinegar, stirring, until it has dissolved. Add the red colouring, if using, and pour over the ginger to cover completely; swivel the jar to expel any air bubbles. Cover with a vinegar-proof lid and seal (see pages 12-13). Store in a cool, dark, dry place, or in the refrigerator, for at least 2 weeks before eating. This will keep for up to 3 months.

Traditionally served in a tiny pile with sushi and sashimi, pickled ginger also goes well with other seafood dishes, especially grilled salmon, and with poultry. It can also be added, finely diced, to salads and it is good to nibble as a refreshing palate cleanser between dishes.

Ginger Wine

MAKES 450ML/16FL OZ

15cm/6in piece of fresh ginger, chopped
450ml/16fl oz rice wine

Put the ginger in a clean, dry bottle or a jar. Pour over the rice wine, cover and leave in a warm place for at least 2 weeks, shaking the jar occasionally, before drinking. Strain the wine when it has reached the flavour intensity you like, or top up with more wine once some has been drunk. This wine will keep indefinitely.

Drink it on its own or add it to salad dressings, stir-fries or fruit salads. You can also use it as a marinade for chicken.

Ginger and Peach Chutney

This is a lively fruit chutney with just a hint of spice. The combination of peaches, ginger and spices makes for a tangy and refreshing blend of flavours.

MAKES ABOUT 1.5G/3½LB

1kg/2¼lb peaches, peeled, quartered
 and stoned
570ml/1 pint white wine vinegar
225g/8oz light soft brown sugar
175g/6oz stem ginger, chopped
115g/4oz stoned dried dates, chopped
115g/4oz plump raisins
115g/4oz flaked almonds
2 onions, finely chopped
3 plump garlic cloves, chopped
grated zest and juice of 2 oranges
1 teaspoon ground allspice
1 teaspoon ground cinnamon
2 teaspoons sea salt

Put all the ingredients in a pan and heat gently, stirring, until the sugar has dissolved. Bring to the boil, then cover and simmer for about 1½ hours, stirring frequently, until there is no free liquid and the chutney is quite thick.

Carefully ladle the chutney into warm, clean, dry jars, then cover with vinegar-proof lids and seal (see pages 12-13). Store in a cool, dark, dry place for at least 2 months before eating.

This chutney is excellent with ripe Camembert and hard cheeses, and makes a good accompaniment to smoked chicken or hot or cold roast chicken, as well as lamb, pork, ham, gammon and game.

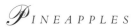

Spiced Pineapple Chutney

Using only fresh fruit produces a really fruity-tasting chutney with a lightly spicy flavour.

MAKES ABOUT 675G/1½LB

2 pineapples, total weight about 1.2kg/2lb 10oz
115ml/4fl oz white wine vinegar
1 teaspoon ground cinnamon
1 teaspoon cardamom seeds
2 teaspoons curry powder
½ teaspoon ground ginger
½ teaspoon ground cloves
175g/6oz sugar

Toast the cardamom seeds in a heavy-based, preferably non-stick, frying pan for ½-1 minute over a low heat, stirring to prevent them from burning, until fragrant. Remove the seeds and crush them with a pestle or the end of a rolling-pin. Set aside.

Peel the pineapples, taking care to remove all the 'eyes'. Slice the pineapple, cut out the core and chop the flesh quite finely, collecting any juices that come out during the preparation.

Put any juices, the vinegar and spices in a saucepan and bring to the boil, then simmer gently for 5 minutes. Add the pineapple and simmer for about 20 minutes until tender.

Over a low heat, stir in the sugar until it has dissolved, then raise the heat and boil, stirring occasionally, until the chutney is thick and there is no free liquid.

Ladle the chutney into warm, clean, dry jars. Cover with vinegar-proof lids and seal (see pages 12-13). Store in a cool, dark, dry place for 1 month before eating.

Right: Spiced Pineapple Chutney combines well with hot and cold gammon, pork, turkey, chicken and cheese.

$\mathscr{A}$ PPLES AND $\mathscr{P}$ EARS

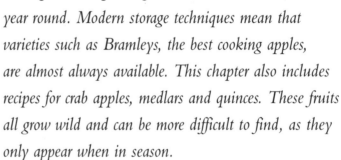

Late summer and autumn, when the pear and apple crops were picked from laden trees in orchards and gardens, were traditionally prime times for preserving. Now, not only do fewer people have their own apple and pear trees, but the fruits are imported in quantity all year round. Modern storage techniques mean that varieties such as Bramleys, the best cooking apples, are almost always available. This chapter also includes recipes for crab apples, medlars and quinces. These fruits all grow wild and can be more difficult to find, as they only appear when in season.

Left (from left to right): Apple Honey; Apple, Citrus and Whisky Mincemeat; Mulled Pears and Curried Apple and Carrot Chutney.

Apple and Cherry Jam

To overcome the problem of getting cherry jam to set, because cherries have such a low pectin content, the cherries are sometimes cooked in redcurrant juice, which is high in natural pectin. Here, however, I have used the juice of cooking apples (by preference, Bramleys), as they are more abundant and cheaper than redcurrants, the flavour of the two fruits goes well together, and the jam looks attractive.

MAKES ABOUT 2KG/4½LB

**675g/1½lb sharp, juicy cooking apples,
 preferably Bramleys
1.4kg/3lb sharp cooking cherries, such as
 Morello or Duke, stoned
2½ tablespoons lemon juice
1.2kg/2lb 10oz warmed sugar (see page 7)**

Slice the apples without peeling or coring them, then cook very gently in 570ml/1 pint water in a covered pan for about 30 minutes, stirring occasionally, until they are very soft. Tip the contents of this pan into a scalded jelly bag suspended over a bowl and leave to strain, undisturbed, in a cool place for 6-8 hours to make 300ml/10fl oz juice.

Gently simmer the apple juice, cherries and lemon juice for about 30 minutes until much of the water from the mixture has been evaporated.

Remove the pan from the heat, stir in the sugar, then return to the heat and cook gently, stirring, until the sugar has dissolved. Raise the heat and boil hard for about 10 minutes, stirring as necessary, until setting point is reached (see page 17).

Remove from the heat and skim any scum from the surface with a slotted spoon. Pour the jam into warm, clean, dry jars. Cover and seal (see pages 12-13). Leave over-night to set. Store in a cool, dark, dry place.

Right: Apple and Cherry Puffs are discs of melt-in-the-mouth pastry filled with fruity jam.

Apple and Cherry Puffs

Made from soft cheese and without any water, the pastry in this recipe is meltingly light and 'short'.

MAKES 12

**115g/4oz unsalted butter, softened
115g/4oz unsalted full-fat soft cheese
few drops of almond essence
150g/5oz plain flour
Apple and Cherry Jam (see left)**

In a bowl, beat the butter, cheese and essence together, then gradually beat in the flour. Form into a ball, wrap in greaseproof paper or cling film and chill for 1 hour.

Preheat the oven to 200°C/400°F/gas mark 6. On a lightly floured surface, roll out the pastry and cut into twelve 7.5cm/3in circles. Place a large teaspoonful of jam on each circle, fold the pastry in half and press the edges together to seal. Transfer to a baking sheet and bake for about 15 minutes until pale gold. Serve hot with crème fraîche.

A PPLES

Apple Honey

Adding apples and spices to an inexpensive honey transforms it into a luxurious-tasting spread. Either cooking or eating apples can be used, provided the latter are crisp, juicy and not too sweet.

MAKES ABOUT 1.4KG/3LB

**1.4kg/3lb cooking or eating apples, chopped
  without peeling or coring
Per 570ml/1pint of juice:
350g/12oz sugar
115g/4oz clear honey
5cm/2in cinnamon stick
3 cloves
small piece of fresh ginger**

Put the apples and 850ml/1½ pints water in a saucepan and cook for 20-30 minutes until soft and pulpy, stirring occasionally. Tip the mixture into a scalded jelly bag suspended over a non-metallic bowl and leave to strain, undisturbed, in a cool place for 8-12 hours.

Measure the apple juice, then pour it into the rinsed pan. For each 570ml/1 pint juice add 350g/12oz sugar and 115g/4oz honey, as well as a cinnamon stick, 3 cloves and a small piece of ginger (tied in a muslin bag), and heat gently, stirring, until the sugar has dissolved. Raise the heat and boil hard for about 4 minutes until setting point is reached (see page 17).

Remove from the heat, skim any scum from the surface with a slotted spoon and discard the spice bag. Pour the honey into warm, clean, dry jars. Cover and seal (see pages 12-13). Once set, this is ready to eat. Store in a cool, dark, dry place.

Stir into Greek yogurt, fromage frais or cream; spoon on to pancakes, Scotch pancakes or waffles; spread on bread, toast or slices of plain cake; spoon on to plain steamed puddings or stir into milk puddings.

Caramelized Apple Jam

Remove the pan from the heat once the caramel reaches the golden stage as it can quickly turn bitter if it continues cooking.

MAKES ABOUT 1.8KG/4LB

**2.2kg/5lb cooking apples, preferably Bramleys
juice of 1 lemon
1kg/2¼lb sugar
4 tablespoons brandy or Calvados**

Peel, core (see page 56) and dice the apples, then toss them in a bowl with the lemon juice to prevent discoloration.

Stir 450g/1lb sugar and 4 tablespoons water together in a saucepan over a low heat and bring slowly to the boil. Cook until golden brown, then quickly remove from the heat and immediately stir in the apples to mix well with the caramel (see below). The caramel will harden on contact with the apples, but will melt again once heated. (Beware of scalding steam at this point.)

Add the remaining sugar, stirring until the sugar has dissolved. Return the mixture to a low heat and bring very slowly back to the boiling point, stirring frequently. Continue cooking for about 10-15 minutes until the apples are very soft and some of the liquid

Adding the apples: *as soon as the caramel has turned a light brown colour, remove from the heat, tip in the diced apples and stir in well.*

has boiled away, then press them through a non-metallic sieve with a wooden spoon and return to the pan. If the purée is already very thick, boil for another minute, but if it is thin, boil again until reduced and thickened.

Remove pan from the heat and stir in the brandy. Spoon into warm, clean, dry jars. Cover and seal (see pages 12-13). Leave overnight. Store in a cool, dark, dry place.

Apple Nectar

Cool glasses of Apple Nectar on a summer's day are just what the doctor ordered.

MAKES ABOUT 1.7 LITRES/3 PINTS

**3 cloves
1.4kg/3lb cooking apples, peeled, quartered
  and cored (see page 56) to make about
  1kg/2¼lb
400g/14oz sugar
juice of 1 lemon**

Tie the cloves in a muslin bag and put in a pan with the apples and 300ml/10fl oz water. Cover and cook gently for about 30 minutes, stirring occasionally, until the apples are tender. Discard the muslin bag then purée the apples in a blender or push the flesh through a non-metallic sieve.

In a saucepan, gently heat the sugar in 450ml/15fl oz water, stirring until dissolved. Raise the heat, then add the lemon juice and boil for 2 minutes. Stir in the purée and simmer for 10 minutes, stirring occasionally.

Adjust the heat if necessary so that the nectar is gently bubbling, and ladle into warm, clean, dry bottles. Cover and seal (see pages 12-13). This will keep in a cool, dark, dry place for about 4 months. Shake the bottle before pouring.

Serve chilled on its own, or with sweet biscuits or cake; add to fruit salads.

A PPLES

Spiced Apple and Cider Butter

For this butter, use a well-flavoured variety of eating apple for taste, and sharp cooking apples, with perhaps some crab apples, for tartness. The amount of lemon juice needed will depend on the sweetness of the apples.

MAKES ABOUT 1.1KG/2½LB

1.1 litres/2 pints dry cider
675g/1½lb cooking apples, such as Bramleys, peeled, cored (see page 56) and sliced
675g/1½lb well-flavoured eating apples, peeled, cored and sliced
grated zest and juice of 1 thin-skinned lemon
warmed sugar (see page 7)
½ teaspoon ground cinnamon
½ teaspoon freshly grated nutmeg

Pour the cider into a pan and boil hard for 15 minutes until reduced by half. Add the apples and lemon zest and juice, cover the pan, and cook for 20-30 minutes until very soft and reduced to a purée, stirring occasionally to make sure the apples cook evenly and to break them up. Press the contents of the pan through a non-metallic sieve into a bowl.

Weigh the purée and return it to the rinsed pan. Add 175g/6oz sugar for every 350g/12oz purée, the cinnamon and nutmeg and stir over a low heat until the sugar has dissolved. Then boil gently for 35-45 minutes, stirring occasionally and then more frequently, until the stirring is constant and the mixture has the consistency of thick double cream.

Spoon into warm, clean, dry jars. Cover and seal (see pages 12-13). Store in a cool, dark, dry place for a few days before eating.

Spiced Apple and Cider Butter makes a good base for thickly sliced apples in an open apple tart.

Spiced Apple and Orange Jelly

I make this jelly in winter partly because no seasonal ingredients are called for, and partly because its warm, spicy, tangy flavour seems more appropriate for winter days and winter meals.

MAKES ABOUT 1.1KG/2½LB

675g/1½lb cooking apples, preferably Bramleys, chopped without peeling and coring
4 large oranges, chopped
1 large lemon, chopped
1 cinnamon stick
25g/1oz unpeeled fresh ginger, sliced
warmed sugar (see page 7)

Put all the ingredients, except the sugar, in a pan and add 1.75 litres/3 pints water. Bring to the boil, then cover and simmer gently, stirring occasionally, for about 1 hour or until the fruit is soft.

Tip the contents of the pan into a scalded jelly bag suspended over a non-metallic bowl and leave to strain, undisturbed, in a cool place for 8-12 hours.

Measure the juice and pour it back into the rinsed pan. Add 450g/1lb sugar for every 570ml/1 pint juice and heat gently, stirring, until the sugar has dissolved, then boil hard for about 10 minutes until setting point is reached (see page 17).

Remove the pan from the heat and skim away any scum with a slotted spoon. Pour into warm, clean, dry jars. Cover and seal (see pages 12-13). Leave overnight to set. Store in a cool, dark, dry place.

Variation: *Spiced Apple Jelly*
Use 2kg/1½lb cooking apples, such as Bramleys, 2 sliced lemons, 25g/1oz sliced fresh ginger, 1 cinnamon stick, ½ teaspoon cloves, 200ml/7fl oz white wine vinegar and 1.75 litres/3 pints water. Follow the method above.

Apple, Citrus and Whisky Mincemeat

This is a moist, tangy, spicy mincemeat.

MAKES 1.8KG/4LB

550g/1¼lb Bramley apples, peeled, cored (see page 56) and chopped
15g/½oz butter
115g/4oz dried apricots, chopped
225g/8oz sultanas
225g/8oz seedless raisins
225g/8oz dark muscovado sugar
115g/4oz currants
115g/4oz mixed peel
75g/3oz hazelnuts, skinned and coarsely chopped
75g/3oz blanched almonds, coarsely chopped
grated zest and juice of 1 orange
grated zest and juice of 1 lemon
1 teaspoon ground cinnamon
½ teaspoon ground ginger
½ teaspoon freshly grated nutmeg
pinch of ground cloves
115g/4oz vegetarian or beef suet
150ml/5fl oz whisky

Gently cook the apples with 4 tablespoons water and the butter in a covered saucepan for about 20 minutes until soft and pulpy. Remove the lid, raise the heat and cook, stirring, for about 10 minutes, until almost all the liquid has evaporated. Leave to cool.

Stir the remaining ingredients together in a large non-metallic bowl. Stir in the apple. Cover and leave overnight in a cool place.

The next day, give the mincemeat a good stir then pack it firmly into clean, dry jars, taking care not to trap any air bubbles. Cover and seal (see pages 12-13). Store in a cool, dark, dry place for at least 6 weeks before using.

Serve with poached orange slices or use as a filling for short-crust pastry pies.

𝒜PPLES

Minted Apple Relish

Vary the flavour of this relish by using different types of mint – spearmint is the most common garden mint, but you can also try apple, lemon, pineapple or ginger mint.

MAKES ABOUT 900G/2LB

225g/8oz onions, sliced
2 teaspoons dry English mustard powder
1 teaspoon black peppercorns
1 cinnamon stick, broken in half
¼ teaspoon ground mace
1 teaspoon sea salt
225g/8oz sugar
300ml/10fl oz Spiced Vinegar (see page 139)
675g/1½lb cooking apples, preferably
 Bramleys, peeled, cored (see page 56)
 and thinly sliced
15g/½oz fresh mint, finely chopped

Put all the ingredients, except the apples and mint, in a saucepan and heat gently, stirring until the sugar has dissolved. Bring to the boil, then simmer gently for 10 minutes. Stir in the apples and continue cooking for a further 10 minutes or until the apples are tender but still retain their shape.

Remove the mixture from the heat and leave to cool. Remove the cinnamon and pack the relish into clean, dry jars, sprinkling mint between the layers, taking care not to trap any air pockets. Cover with vinegar-proof lids and seal (see pages 12-13). Store in a cool, dark, dry place for at least 1 month before eating.

Use as a stuffing for a boned leg or shoulder of lamb; stir into freshly cooked new potatoes and leave to cool, then serve as a salad; serve with smoked pork loin or smoked chicken.

Curried Apple and Carrot Chutney

Fresh horseradish enlivens this chutney.

MAKES ABOUT 1.1KG/2½LB

600g/1¼lb cooking apples, such as Bramleys,
 peeled, cored (see page 56) and chopped
250g/9oz carrots, thinly sliced lengthways
1 onion, sliced
115g/4oz raisins
115g/4oz fresh horseradish, grated
1 tablespoon curry powder
1 tablespoon ground ginger
1 teaspoon mustard seeds
300ml/10fl oz cider vinegar
225g/8oz soft light brown sugar
2 teaspoons sea salt

Stir all the ingredients together in a pan and heat gently, stirring constantly, until the sugar has dissolved. Bring to the boil, then simmer, stirring frequently for about 30-45 minutes, until the ingredients are tender, the chutney is thick and there is no free liquid.

Spoon the chutney into warm, clean, dry jars, taking care not to trap any air bubbles. Cover with vinegar-proof lids and seal (see pages 12-13). Store in a cool, dark, dry place for at least 2 months before eating.

Serve as an accompaniment to spicy northern Indian dishes.

Below: if you grow your own apples and mint, Minted Apple Relish can be a very cheap preserve to produce.

Uncooked Apple Chutney

This simple chutney couldn't be easier or quicker to make.

MAKES ABOUT 1KG/2¼LB

225g/8oz sultanas
1 tablespoon chopped fresh ginger
25g/1oz brown mustard seeds
225g/8oz demerara sugar
2 teaspoons sea salt
300ml/10fl oz cider vinegar
675g/1½lb cooking apples, peeled, cored
 (see below) and coarsely chopped
225g/8oz onion, very finely chopped
2 garlic cloves, very finely chopped (optional)

Stir the sultanas, ginger, mustard seeds, sugar, salt and vinegar together in a non-metallic bowl until the sugar has dissolved.

Stir in the apples, onion and garlic, if using. Cover and leave in a cool place for 1 week, stirring once every day.

Spoon the chutney into clean, dry jars, taking care not to trap any air bubbles. Cover with vinegar-proof lids and seal (see pages 12-13). This chutney is now ready to eat. Store in a cool, dark, dry place. Keep

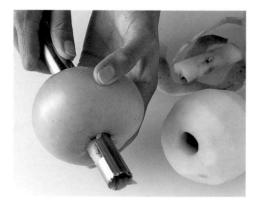

Coring apples: an apple corer is the quickest, easiest and most effective way of removing the cores from apples and other fruits.

the chutney closely covered to make sure it doesn't dry out.

———

Stir into the skimmed pan juices from roast pork or dark game birds and serve with the meat. It is also good with a Wensleydale or Lancashire cheese ploughman's lunch.

Crab Apple and Clove Jelly

Crab apples are too hard and astringent to eat raw and too small to peel and core. Making a jelly is therefore an ideal way of using them. Cloves bring out the warm, spicy note in their flavour.

MAKES ABOUT 1.5-1.8KG/3½-4LB

2.5kg/5½lb crab apples
6 cloves
warmed sugar (see page 7)

Chop the crab apples without peeling or coring them and put them into a pan with the cloves and 1.75 litres/3 pints water. Bring to the boil, then cover and simmer for about 1¼ hours, stirring occasionally until soft and pulpy.

Tip the contents of the pan into a scalded jelly bag suspended over a large non-metallic bowl and leave to strain, undisturbed, in a cool place for 8-12 hours. Measure the juice and pour into the rinsed pan. Add 450g/1lb sugar for every 570ml/1 pint juice and heat gently, stirring, until the sugar has dissolved. Raise the heat and boil hard for about 10 minutes until setting point is reached (see page 17). Remove the mixture from the heat and skim the scum from the surface with a slotted spoon. Pour the jelly into warm, clean, dry jars. Cover and seal (see pages 12-13). Leave overnight to set. Store in a cool, dark, dry place.

Mulled Pears

Use a soft fruity wine such as a Loire red like Chinon, or a Beaujolais, rather than more robust types, such as young Cabernet Sauvignon wines.

MAKES ABOUT 1.75 LITRES/2½ PINTS

1.4kg/3lb small under-ripe pears, such as
 Conference
cloves
7.5cm/3in cinnamon stick, broken into pieces
2 blades of mace
7.5cm/3in piece fresh ginger, chopped
zest of 1 small lemon, cut into thin strips
225g/8oz sugar
about ¾ bottle red wine

Preheat the oven to 130°C/250°F/gas mark ½.

Carefully peel the pears, leaving the stalks intact. Stud each pear with a clove, then divide them between two 1 litre/1¾ pint and one 500ml/18fl oz jars. Distribute the spices, ginger, lemon zest, sugar and wine between the jars, making sure the pears are covered with liquid. Cover but do not seal the jars. Put in the oven for 3 hours. Remove and seal the jars (see pages 12-13). Once cool, store in a cool, dark, dry place.

Variation: *Cherries in Red Wine*
Gently heat 225g/8oz sugar in 570ml/1 pint red wine until dissolved, then add 2 fresh bay leaves and simmer for 10 minutes until syrupy. Add 900g/2lb cherries and cook gently until the cherries are tender. Pour into a clear, warm, dry jar, discarding the bay leaves. Cover and seal. Makes about 1¾ litres/2½ pints.

———

Serve very cold with crème caramel or rice pudding; use in clafoutis or open tarts (see opposite); or serve with roast duck, venison or hare, deglazing the cooking juices with some of the syrup and lemon juice.

Mulled Pear Tart

SERVES 4-6

175g/6oz plain flour
pinch of salt
50g/2oz icing sugar, sifted
115g/4oz unsalted butter, softened
1 egg yolk, size 3
1 tablespoon cold water
250ml/9fl oz mixed milk and cream
1 vanilla pod
3 egg yolks, size 1
50g/2oz sugar
25g/1oz mixed plain flour and cornflour
15g/½oz unsalted butter, diced
about 150ml/5fl oz juice from the Mulled Pears
10 Mulled Pears (see page 56), halved

Sift the flour and salt on to a work surface
and make a well in the centre. Put the icing
sugar, butter, egg yolk and water into the
well and pinch them together to make a
paste, then draw in the flour to form a ball.
Put on a plate, cover and chill for 2 hours.

Roll out the pastry and use to line a
loose-bottomed 22.5cm/9in fluted flan tin,
pressing the pastry well into the sides and
base. Run the rolling pin over the top to cut
off excess pastry. Chill for 20 minutes.

Meanwhile, preheat the oven to 200°C/
400°F/gas mark 6. Prick the base of the
pastry case, line with grease-proof paper
and weight down with baking beans. Bake
for about 12 minutes, then lower the oven
temperature to 190°C/375°F/gas mark 5.
Remove the paper and beans from the
pastry case and bake for a further 8-10
minutes until the pastry is pale gold. Leave
to cool on a wire rack.

To make the crème pâtissière, gently heat
the milk and cream and the vanilla pod to
simmering point, remove from the heat,
cover and leave for 30 minutes. Whisk the
egg yolks and sugar in a bowl until thick. Sift
the flour and cornflour into the egg mixture
and beat. Boil the milk mixture and strain
into the egg mixture, whisking constantly.

Return the mixture to the pan and bring to
the boil, whisking. Simmer for 2-3 minutes.
Remove from the heat, stir in the butter and
pour into a bowl. Leave to cool, stirring
occasionally, then cover and chill.

Boil the juice from the pears until syrupy

*Above: brushing with reduced pear liquid adds
colour to this meltingly spicy Mulled Pear Tart.*

and leave to cool. Fill the pastry case with
the crème pâtissière. Lay the pears on top
and brush with the syrupy liquid.

Pear Chutney

When making this extremely simple recipe, I sometimes use chopped stoned prunes or currants instead of raisins, or add chopped onions or some allspice.

MAKES 1.5-1.8KG/3½-4LB

1.4kg/3lb firm-ripe pears, cored and chopped but not peeled
2 large garlic cloves, finely chopped
2 teaspoons sea salt
1-2 teaspoons cayenne pepper, to taste
2 teaspoons freshly ground coriander
2 tablespoons chopped fresh ginger
225g/8oz plump raisins
225ml/8fl oz white wine vinegar and lime juice, mixed in equal quantities
200g/7oz warmed soft light brown sugar (see page 7)

Put the pears, together with all the ingredients except the sugar, in a large saucepan, cover and simmer for 15 minutes, stirring occasionally, until the pears are soft.

Add the warmed sugar and stir until dissolved, then bring the mixture to the boil.

The mixture should be a thick soft purée with no free liquid; if it seems too thick, add about 115ml/4fl oz water and boil again for about 10 minutes, stirring, until the right consistency is reached.

Ladle the chutney into warm, clean, dry jars (taking care not to trap any air bubbles). Cover with vinegar-proof lids and seal (see pages 12-13). Store in a cool, dark, dry place for at least 1-2 months before eating.

Pear and Pineapple Conserve

Reserve the juices that come from the pineapple when you are preparing it to add to the cooking liquid.

MAKES 1.1KG/2½LB

675g/1½lb large pineapple, peeled, cored and finely chopped to make 1lb flesh
1kg/2¼lb firm-ripe pears, peeled, cored and thinly sliced
450g/1lb warmed sugar with pectin (see page 7)

Gently cook the pineapple in 225ml/8fl oz water and the reserved pineapple juices in a small covered saucepan for 35-40 minutes until it is just tender. Add the pears and cook gently for a further 20-25 minutes, covered, until both fruits are tender.

Over a low heat, add the sugar and stir until it has dissolved, then boil hard, without stirring, for about 20-30 minutes, until thickened and a light set is reached.

Ladle into warm, clean, dry jars. Cover and seal (see pages 12-13). Leave overnight. Store in a cool, dark, dry place.

Spiced Pears

This recipe puts hard, flavourless pears to very good use.

MAKES 1.1 LITRES/2 PINTS

1.4kg/3lb firm pears, peeled
1 teaspoon allspice berries
2.5cm/1in piece of fresh ginger, sliced
1 teaspoon cloves
2 cinnamon sticks
225g/8oz sugar
450ml/16fl oz white wine vinegar

Halve or quarter the pears. Remove the cores and put the pears in a saucepan with enough water just to cover them. Bring to the boil, then simmer for 5 minutes.

Drain the pears and set aside, reserving the liquid. Make the liquid up to 450ml/16fl oz with water, then pour back into the pan. Add the remaining ingredients, except the pears, and cook over a low heat, stirring until the sugar has dissolved, then simmer for 5 minutes.

Add the pears to the pan and simmer for 20-30 minutes until they are tender and translucent but still hold their shape.

Left (clockwise from right): quinces, Comice pears, Conference pears and William pears.

Quinces, Medlars

Use a slotted spoon to transfer the pears to a warm, clean, dry jar, then pour over the liquid and spices. Cover with a vinegar-proof lid and seal (see pages 12-13). Store in a cool, dark, dry place for at least 1 month before eating.

———————— ☞ ————————

Serve with cold roast pork or cooked tongue; use the spiced vinegar to make salad dressings.

Quince Cheese

The wonderful flavour of the sweetened cooked fruit (it is inedible raw) will permeate fruits cooked with it, so if you do not have enough quinces, combine them with apples and a chopped slice of orange. Use quinces when they are yellow all over.

MAKES ABOUT 1.4KG/3LB

1.4kg/3lb quinces
warmed sugar (see page 7)

Wash the grey down from the quinces, then chop the fruit, including the skins and cores. Put into a large saucepan, just cover with water and simmer gently for about 30-45 minutes until the fruit is tender.

Tip the contents of the pan into a non-metallic sieve over a non-metallic bowl and press through with a wooden spoon. Measure the purée and return to the rinsed-out pan. Add 450g/1lb sugar for each 570ml/1 pint purée and heat gently, stirring, until the sugar has dissolved. Bring the mixture to the boil, then continue to boil, stirring frequently, for 45-55 minutes or until it is so thick that the spoon leaves a clean line when drawn through it.

Spoon into clean, warm, dry jars or lightly-oiled moulds, cover with waxed paper and seal (see pages 12-13). Store in a cool, dark, dry place for 2-3 months before eating.

Medlar Jelly

Medlars are an unusual apple-like fruit which ripen in the late autumn, but remain hard, green, astringent and inedible. However, the fruit browns and softens if bletted – stored in sawdust or straw – for about 1-2 months. If possible, use about two-thirds bletted medlars and one-third firm fruit. Medlars are sold by specialist greengrocers.

MAKES ABOUT 1.1KG/2½LB

900g/2lb medlars, chopped but not peeled
or cored
warmed sugar (see page 7)

Place the medlars in a pan and pour in enough water just to cover them. Bring to the boil, then cover and simmer for 30-45 minutes, stirring occasionally, until the fruit is very soft. Tip the contents of the pan into

Above: this glowing Quince Cheese is delicious eaten with Danish Blue or Stilton cheese.

a scalded jelly bag suspended over a non-metallic bowl and leave to strain, undisturbed, in a cool place for 8-12 hours.

Measure the juice and pour it into a saucepan. Add 450g/1lb sugar for every 570ml/1 pint juice and stir over a low heat until the sugar has dissolved. Raise the heat and boil hard for 10-15 minutes, stirring occasionally, until setting point is reached (see page 17).

Remove the pan from the heat and skim any scum away with a slotted spoon. Ladle the jelly into warm, clean, dry jars. Cover and seal (see pages 12-13). Leave over-night to set. Store in a cool, dark, dry place.

———————— ☞ ————————

Serve with game, lamb, pork or ham.

CITRUS FRUITS

Marmalade is the preserve most obviously associated with citrus fruits and possibly the only one that many people will think of, at least immediately. Indeed, all citrus fruits, and not just oranges, are used for marmalades because their sharp flavours, especially when the peel is included, seem just what is needed for breakfast. Citrus peels harden when cooked with sugar so they must first be completely softened before the sugar is added to the mixture. These fruits have a high pectin content so they set readily and are natural candidates for making jams and jellies. Their fresh, tangy flavour makes them ideal for a whole host of other preserves, ranging from Kumquats or Clementines in Vodka and Cointreau (see page 72) to chutneys, Moroccan Preserved Lemons (see page 75), Indian Sweet-sour Lime Pickle (see page 77) and, typically, English fruit curds. Citrus peel can also be candied for use in baking and as a sweetmeat to eat with coffee after dinner.

Left (from left to right): Orange and Tarragon Jelly, Kumquats in Vodka and Cointreau and Seville Orange Marmalade.

Oxford Marmalade

The characteristic dark colour and deep flavour of traditional Oxford marmalade is the result of long boiling before the sugar is added.

MAKES ABOUT 2.2KG/5LB

675g/1½lb Seville oranges
1.7 litres/3 pints boiling water
1.4kg/3lb warmed sugar (see page 7)

Peel the oranges and cut the peel into chunky strips. Chop the flesh, reserving the pips. Put the flesh and peel strips into a large non-metallic bowl and the pips into a small one. Pour 300ml/10fl oz of the boiling water into the small bowl with the pips and the remainder into the large bowl. Cover both bowls and leave overnight.

Tip the pips into a non-metallic sieve placed over the large bowl, using their water to wash off the soft, clear jelly surrounding them. If necessary, ladle some of the water from the large bowl over the pips to rinse them again; discard the pips.

Tip the contents of the large bowl into a pan, bring to the boil and simmer gently for 2-2½ hours, stirring occasionally, until the peel is very soft – the longer the boiling, the darker the marmalade will be. Top up with more water during boiling if necessary.

Over a gentle heat, stir in the warmed sugar until it has dissolved. Boil gently until the desired colour is reached, then raise the heat and boil hard for a further 15-20 minutes, stirring as necessary, until setting point is reached (see page 17).

Remove the pan from the heat and skim the scum from the marmalade's surface with a slotted spoon. Leave to stand for 10-15 minutes, then stir the marmalade and ladle into warm, clean, dry jars. Cover and seal (see pages 12-13). Leave overnight to set. Store in a cool, dark, dry place.

Leisurely Marmalade

This marmalade is made at a leisurely pace over three days, hence its name.

MAKES ABOUT 1.5KG/2¾LB

6 large sweet oranges
½ large lemon
warmed sugar (see page 7)

Remove the stalk ends from the fruit and discard. Slice the fruit and leave to soak in a covered pan with 500ml/18fl oz water for one day.

The next day, bring the mixture to the boil, then simmer gently, stirring occasionally, for 25-50 minutes or so, depending how soft you want the peel to be. Remove from the heat and leave to cool, then cover and leave for a further day.

Weigh the fruit and juice and return to the pan with 650g/1lb 5oz sugar for every 450g/1lb fruit and juice. Stir to dissolve the sugar, then bring the mixture to the boil and boil hard, stirring as necessary, for about 1 hour until setting point is reached (see page 17).

Remove from the heat and skim the scum from the surface with a slotted spoon. Leave to stand for 10-15 minutes. Stir and ladle into warm, clean, dry jars. Cover and seal (see pages 12-13). Leave overnight to set. Store in a cool, dark, dry place.

Ginger and Apple Marmalade

The ground and preserved ginger in this recipe add warmth to the taste of the marmalade, making it particularly appropriate for winter.

MAKES ABOUT 2.2KG/5LB

225g/8oz Seville oranges
675g/1½lb cooking apples, peeled, cored and chopped
1.6kg/3½lb warmed sugar (see page 7)
2 teaspoons ground ginger
115g/4oz preserved ginger, diced

Peel the oranges and finely shred the peel. Coarsely chop the orange flesh, removing and reserving the membranes, pith and pips. Tie the membranes, pith and pips in a muslin bag with a long length of string. Put the chopped orange, peel, juice, and 1.4 litres/ 2½ pints water in a pan, and tie the muslin bag on the pan handle so the bag is suspended in the mixture. Bring the mixture to the boil, then simmer for 1-1½ hours, stirring occasionally, until the peel is soft and the contents of the pan reduced by half.

Remove the pan from the heat. Scoop out the muslin bag with a slotted spoon and press the bag hard with the back of a metal spoon so that the juices run back into the pan. Discard the bag.

Meanwhile, simmer the apples in 150ml/ 5fl oz water for about 8 minutes until pulpy.

Add the apple pulp, sugar, ground ginger and preserved ginger to the oranges and stir

Above: Seville oranges from Spain are used for making many traditional marmalades.

ORANGES

Marmalade Gingerbread

Instead of adding golden syrup and black treacle to gingerbread I tried adding marmalade, and the result was an outstanding success. This is now the only way I make such cakes. Marmalades I have used are Seville Orange (see pages 18-19), Pineapple and Orange (see page 65), Tangerine (see page 70) and Peach (see page 101), each one giving its own unique character to the gingerbread. This gingerbread is best kept for a couple of days before being eaten.

MAKES A 20-22.5CM/8-9IN ROUND CAKE

225g/8oz butter, diced
225g/8oz soft dark brown sugar
300ml/10fl oz milk
225g/8oz marmalade (see above)
350g/12oz self-raising flour
1½-2 tablespoons ground ginger
2 teaspoons blcarbonate of soda
2 teaspoons ground cinnamon
1 teaspoon freshly grated nutmeg
2 eggs, size 1 or 2, beaten
7 pieces preserved ginger, chopped
115g/4oz plump raisins

Preheat the oven to 160°C/310°F/gas mark 2. Butter a 20-22.5cm/8-9in round cake tin and line the base with greaseproof paper.

In a saucepan, gently heat together the butter, sugar, milk and marmalade, stirring occasionally, until the butter and sugar have melted. Remove from the heat and leave to cool. Stir together the flour, ginger, bicarbonate of soda, cinnamon and nutmeg and form a well in the centre. Slowly pour in the marmalade mixture, stirring the dry ingredients into the liquid to make a smooth batter; add the eggs towards the end. Stir in the chopped ginger and raisins. Pour the mixture into the cake tin and bake for about 1½ hours until risen and firm to the touch in the centre. Leave to cool in the tin. Store in an air-tight container.

until the sugar has dissolved. Raise the heat and boil hard for about 25 minutes, stirring as necessary, until setting point is reached (see page 17).

Remove the pan from the heat and skim the scum from the surface with a slotted spoon. Leave to stand for 10-15 minutes,

Above: Marmalade Gingerbread is a moist cake that will keep well in an air-tight container.

stir to distribute the peel and ginger and ladle into warm, clean, dry jars. Cover and seal (see pages 12-13). Leave overnight to set. Store in a cool, dark, dry place.

Glazed Spare Ribs

These ribs are great for family suppers or informal meals. The best marmalades to use are Ginger and Apple Marmalade (see page 62), Grapefruit, Orange and Lemon Marmalade (see page 65) and Seville Orange Marmalade (see pages 18-19).

SERVES 4

8 tablespoons marmalade (see above)
2 tablespoons clear honey
2 garlic cloves, crushed
300ml/10fl oz dry cider
8 tablespoons soy sauce
3 tablespoons lime juice
freshly ground black pepper
1.8kg/4lb pork spare ribs
lime wedges to garnish

Place all the ingredients, except the pork, in a pan and gently heat together until blended, stirring as necessary. Remove from the heat and leave to cool.

Divide the pork into individual ribs, if necessary, and trim away the excess fat. Put the ribs in a large, non-metallic dish, pour over the cold marmalade mixture, cover and leave in the refrigerator for about 12 hours, turning the ribs occasionally.

Preheat the oven to 190°C/375°F/gas mark 5. Transfer the ribs and marmalade mixture to a roasting tin about 20 minutes before cooking. Cover the roasting tin with kitchen foil and cook the ribs for 1 hour. Uncover the tin and cook for a further hour, basting occasionally, until the ribs are cooked through and the juices run clear if the meat is pierced with the tip of a knife.

Place the roasting tin on the hob and cook over a high heat for about 3-7 minutes, stirring and turning the ribs, until they are coated with a sticky glaze. Serve garnished with lime wedges.

Left: marmalade adds a delicious tang to the Chinese-style marinade for Glazed Spare Ribs.

Grapefruit, Orange and Lemon Marmalade

This marmalade can be made whenever you feel like it because it contains fruits that are readily available throughout the year.

MAKES ABOUT 2.25KG/5LB

225g/8oz sweet oranges
2 lemons
225g/8oz grapefruit
1.6kg/3lb warmed sugar (see page 7)

Cut the oranges and lemons in half, squeeze out the juice and pour into a pan; reserve the pips and peel. Remove the membranes from the orange and lemon peel and also any excessive amount of pith on any of the peel. Score the grapefruit peel into quarters then remove it and reserve. Chop the grapefruit flesh, reserving the pips, coarse membranes and pith. Add the flesh to the pan. Tie all the membranes, pith and pips in a muslin bag with a long length of string. Tie the end of the string to the pan handle so the bag is suspended in the mixture.

Shred all the peel and add to the pan with 1.7 litres/3 pints water. Bring the mixture to the boil, then simmer gently for about 2 hours until the peel is tender and the contents of the pan reduced by about half.

Using a slotted spoon, scoop out the muslin bag and press the bag hard with the back of a metal spoon so that the juice runs back into the pan. Discard the bag.

Over a low heat, stir in the warmed sugar until it has dissolved. Raise the heat and boil hard for about 15 minutes, stirring as necessary, until setting point is reached (see page 17).

Remove from the heat and skim any scum from the surface with a slotted spoon. Leave to stand for 10-15 minutes, then stir and ladle into warm, clean, dry jars. Cover and seal (see pages 12-13). Leave overnight to set. Store in a cool, dark, dry place.

Pineapple and Orange Marmalade

The addition of pineapple to a simple marmalade makes it rather special.

MAKES ABOUT 1.4KG/3LB

2 sweet oranges, ends removed and thinly sliced
1 lemon, ends removed and thinly sliced
675g/1½lb pineapple, peeled, cored and chopped to produce 450g/1lb flesh
900g/2lb warmed sugar (see page 7)

Cut the orange and lemon slices into quarters or eighths and reserve the pips. Tie the pips in a muslin bag with a long length of string and put the bag into a pan with the orange and lemon pieces and the pineapple, tying the end of the string to the handle so the bag is suspended in the pan. Just cover with water and bring to the boil, then cover the pan and simmer for 35-45 minutes until the fruit and peel are tender.

Scoop out the muslin bag with a slotted spoon and press the bag hard with the back of a metal spoon so that the juices run back into the pan. Discard the bag.

Over a low heat, stir in the sugar until it has dissolved, then raise the heat and boil

Preparing pineapples: *remove the core and all the 'eyes' from the pineapple before cutting the flesh into evenly-sized pieces.*

hard for 10-15 minutes, stirring as necessary, until setting point is reached (see page 17).

Remove from the heat and skim the scum from the surface with a slotted spoon. Leave to stand for 10-15 minutes, then stir and ladle into warm, clean, dry jars. Cover and seal (see pages 12-13). Leave overnight to set. Store in a cool, dark, dry place.

Rhubarb and Orange Chutney

Dried figs give this chutney an unusual taste.

MAKES ABOUT 1.8KG/4LB

450g/1lb rhubarb, finely chopped
225g/8oz onions, finely chopped
grated zest and juice of 1 orange
175g/6oz dried figs, quite finely chopped
50g/2oz plump raisins
450g/1lb sugar
425ml/15fl oz Spiced Vinegar (see page 139)
1½ teaspoons brown mustard seeds
½-¾ teaspoon allspice berries
1½ teaspoons black peppercorns, crushed

Put all the ingredients, except the spices, in a pan. Tie the spices in a muslin bag with a long length of string and add to the pan, tying the string to the handle so the bag is suspended in the mixture. Heat gently, stirring, until the sugar has dissolved. Bring the mixture to the boil, then simmer gently, stirring occasionally, for 1 hour until the chutney is thick and no free liquid is visible.

Scoop out the muslin bag with a slotted spoon and press the bag hard with the back of a metal spoon so that the juices run back into the pan. Discard the bag. Ladle the chutney into warm, clean, dry jars, taking care not to trap any air bubbles. Cover with vinegar-proof lids and seal (see pages 12-13). Store in a cool, dark, dry place for 2 months before eating.

Pickled Orange Wedges

I like to have a jar of these wedges in the pantry. This is such an easy recipe to make, that when I have some suitable oranges, I usually pickle a few in this way.

MAKES 1.3KG/3LB

4 plump, thin-skinned oranges
450g/1lb sugar
12 cloves
15g/½oz piece fresh ginger, chopped
7.5cm/3in cinnamon stick
15g/½oz allspice berries
570ml/1 pint white wine vinegar

Cut each orange into 8-12 segments; discard the pips. Put the segments into a flameproof casserole, just cover with water and simmer for 45-60 minutes until the orange peels are tender, but be careful not to overcook the fruit.

Meanwhile, gently heat the sugar, cloves, ginger, cinnamon and allspice berries in the vinegar, stirring until the sugar has dissolved. Raise the heat and bring the mixture to the boil, then simmer for 10 minutes, stirring as necessary.

Preheat the oven to 140°C/275°F/gas mark 1.

Strain off and discard the liquid from the casserole, then replace it with the hot vinegar. Cover the casserole and put it in the oven for about 1 hour, until the orange peels are translucent.

Using a slotted spoon, transfer the oranges to warm, clean, dry jars and keep warm in the turned-off oven.

Boil the vinegar for about 10 minutes, until it is beginning to thicken, then pour over the oranges to cover completely. Swivel the jars to expel any air bubbles. Distribute the spices between the jars, breaking the cinnamon as necessary. Cover with vinegar-proof lids and seal (see pages 12-13). Store in a cool, dark, dry place for at least 2 months before eating.

Serve with pork or game pies; hot or cold roast pork, gammon, ham, game or goose; grilled, fried or roast duck; for hot dishes, deglaze the cooking juices with a little of the spiced vinegar.

Honey-spiced Pickled Oranges

Honey adds a special flavour that combines well with the orange, spices and white wine vinegar in this pickle.

MAKES ABOUT 1.4KG/3LB

6 oranges, cut into 0.5cm/¼in slices
1 cinnamon stick
1 teaspoon coriander seeds
1 teaspoon cardamom seeds
½ teaspoon black peppercorns, crushed
½ teaspoon cloves
225g/8oz sugar
225g/8oz clear honey
300ml/10fl oz white wine vinegar

Put the orange slices in a saucepan and cover them with water, cover the pan and bring to the boil, then simmer for 30 minutes. Drain the orange slices well.

Heat the cinnamon, the coriander and cardamom seeds in a dry heavy-based frying pan until they smell aromatic, moving them gently around the pan to prevent them from catching. Remove from the heat, then lightly crush the seeds using a pestle and mortar or a small blender. Put all the spices in a pan. Add the sugar, honey and vinegar and heat gently, stirring, until the sugar and honey have dissolved. Raise the heat and bring to the boil, then simmer for 10 minutes.

Add the orange slices and return the mixture to the boil, then cover and simmer for about 20 minutes, until the orange slices are translucent. Using a slotted spoon,

transfer the slices into warm, clean, dry jars. Add the spices and cover with the vinegar. Cover the jars immediately with vinegar-proof lids and seal (see pages 12-13). Store in a cool, dark, dry place for at least 1 month before eating.

Spiced Candied Orange Peel

Any home-made candied peel is far better to eat than all but the most special, and costly, bought peels, and giving your peel a spicy flavour makes it stand out even more. Leaving the peel in large pieces keeps it deliciously moist.

6 oranges, lemons, grapefruit or limes,
 or a mixture
350g/12oz sugar
6 cloves
1 cinnamon stick

Halve or quarter the fruit and remove the peels in single pieces. Simmer the peels in a little water for 1-2 hours, stirring occasionally, until tender. Change the water 2 or 3 times when cooking grapefruit peel. Drain and reserve the water and make it up to 300ml/10fl oz with fresh water.

Pour the water into a clean pan, add 225g/8oz of the sugar and the cloves and cinnamon stick and heat gently, stirring, until the sugar has dissolved. Raise the heat and bring the mixture to the boil, then stir in the peels. Remove the pan from the heat and leave in a cool place for 2 days.

Drain the syrup into a clean pan, add the remaining sugar and stir over a low heat until the sugar has dissolved. Add the peel and simmer for 1-1½ hours until transparent. Tip the contents of the pan into a non-metallic bowl, cover and leave in a cool place for approximately 2-3 weeks.

 RANGES

Drain off the syrup and transfer the peel to a wire rack placed over a tray. Put in a warm place or in the oven at no hotter than 50°C/126°F/lowest gas setting, and leave for several hours until it is dry and no longer feels sticky.

Carefully pack the fruit into containers, laying waxed paper or parchment between each layer. Store in a cool, dark, dry place for up to 1 year.

Variation: to make plain candied peel, simply omit the spices and follow the method above.

Orange Curd with Candied Orange Peel

Tangy pieces of home-made candied peel, either spiced or plain, make an interesting texture change in this smooth buttery curd. If you do not have time to make the Candied Orange Peel, you can use shop-bought candied peel.

MAKES ABOUT 675G/1½LB

grated zest and juice of 4 large oranges
115g/4oz Candied Orange Peel (see page 66),
 chopped
225g/8oz unsalted butter, diced
175g/6oz caster sugar
6 egg yolks, size 3

Put the orange zest and orange juice, the candied orange peel, butter and sugar in a heat-proof bowl and place over a saucepan of gently simmering water; do not allow the bottom of the bowl to sit in the water. Heat the mixture gently, stirring constantly, until all the sugar has dissolved and the butter has melted.

Strain the egg yolks into the bowl and continue to stir the mixture over gently simmering water until the curd thickens.

This should take 30-40 minutes. Stir the mixture occasionally at first but more frequently as the cooking progresses and constantly towards the end of the cooking so the curd cooks evenly and does not curdle. The water must not boil.

Pour the curd into warm, clean, dry jars. Cover and seal (see pages 12-13). Store in a cool, dark, dry place or in the refrigerator. Refrigerate the curd after opening.

Above: Orange Curd with Candied Orange Peel makes a delicious buttery spread that is the ideal partner for toasted white bread.

Honeyed Peel

This is somewhat easier and quicker to make than candied peel (see page 66).

MAKES ABOUT 600G/21OZ

about 150g/5oz citrus peel
450g/1lb clear honey

Scrape all the white pith off the peel then cut the peel into strips. Blanch the peel strips in boiling water for 5 minutes. Drain and rinse under running cold water, then dry thoroughly on paper towels.

Make a layer of peel in a clean, dry jar and pour over 1 tablespoon honey. Repeat the layering until all the peel and honey have been used.

Close the jar tightly and store in a cool, dark, dry place for 3 months, shaking the jar occasionally and topping up with more honey, if necessary, so the peel remains covered.

Wherever you would use candied peel in puddings, cakes and biscuits, in rice pudding and ice cream; mix with dried fruit as a stuffing for baked apples; add to apple or pear pies or tarts.

Orange Peel Scrolls

The luxurious taste of this sweet-tangy preserve belies its simplicity and cheapness – in fact, it makes use of the peel, an ingredient that is usually thrown away.

250g/9oz thin orange peel, cut into strips
250g/9oz sugar
1 teaspoon lemon juice

Place the peel in a saucepan with 250ml/ 9fl oz water to cover, and simmer for 40 minutes until it is soft. Drain well, reserving

the water. When cool enough to handle, roll up each strip of orange peel and thread it on to a length of thread knotted at one end, pushing them together so they do not unroll (see below). When all the scrolls are in place, knot the thread again. Add the sugar and lemon juice to the water and heat gently in the pan, stirring until the sugar has dissolved. Raise the heat and bring the mixture to the boil, then add the string of orange peel and simmer for 1 hour until the syrup has been thoroughly absorbed into the peel, and the peel is translucent.

Remove the string of peel, cut one knot, then, using a fork, push the scrolls from the thread into a warm, clean, dry jar. If necessary, boil the syrup hard until it is thick enough to coat the back of a spoon (keep the jar warm in a low oven or on the hob while doing this). Pour the syrup into the jar to cover the peel coils completely. Cover and keep for 1-2 days before eating. Store in a cool, dark, dry place for 6-12 months.

Serve the scrolls and some of the syrup with cream, Greek yogurt or fromage frais and plain sponge fingers or crisp biscuits; serve with creamy or chocolate desserts; roll in granulated sugar and serve with coffee.

Making Orange Peel Scrolls: use a needle to string the scrolls on to a thread. Knot both ends of the thread to prevent them from unrolling.

Orange Shrub

A shrub is an old-fashioned, sweetened alcoholic drink. Unless you have some really fruity tasting oranges, use ready-squeezed fresh orange juice (not the longlife variety). Citric acid freshens and lifts the flavour.

MAKES ABOUT 700ML/1¼ PINTS

2 strips of orange zest, chopped
115ml/4fl oz fresh orange juice, lightly warmed
50g/2oz caster sugar
about 1 teaspoon citric acid (optional)
570ml/1 pint white or dark rum or brandy

Put the orange zest in a small saucepan of boiling water. Return the water to the boil for 1 minute, then drain.

Put the orange zest and juice, sugar and citric acid, if using, in a clean, dry bottle and shake to dissolve the sugar. Add the rum or brandy and shake again, then cover and leave in a cool, dark, dry place for 2 weeks or until clear, shaking the bottle daily.

Strain through a double thickness of muslin and pour into a clean, dry bottle. Close the bottle (see pages 12-13) and store in a cool, dark, dry place for 2 months before drinking.

Vin d'Orange

This aperitif comes from southern France where it is sipped leisurely at many a café.

MAKES 1.1 LITRES/2 PINTS

2 large oranges
250g/9oz caster sugar
1 litre/1¾ pints dry white wine
115ml/4fl oz Armagnac

Pare the zest from the oranges, taking care not to include any white pith. Put the zest in a bottle, add the remaining ingredients and close the bottle.

$\mathscr{C}$LEMENTINES

Shake the bottle, then leave it in a sunny or warm place for about 2 weeks, shaking the bottle daily.

Strain the wine through a non-metallic funnel lined with muslin into a clean, dry bottle. Close the bottle (see pages 12-13). The wine is now ready for drinking.

Clementine Ratafia

A ratafia is a fruit liqueur made by steeping fruit in alcohol for a couple of months to produce a deliciously scented sweet drink; the sweetness can be altered by adjusting the amount of sugar.

MAKES ABOUT 570ML/1 PINT

6 clementines
½ teaspoon coriander seeds, lightly crushed
7.5cm/3in cinnamon stick, broken into 3 pieces
425ml/15fl oz vodka, gin or brandy
175-225g/6-8oz caster sugar

Halve the clementines, squeeze the juice from the fruit, then pour it into a clean, dry jar. Pull the flesh and membranes away from the fruit peel and discard them. Cut the peel into thin strips and add to the jar with the coriander seeds, cinnamon pieces, spirit, and sugar to taste.

Cover and seal the jar and shake the ingredients together. Store in a cool, dark, dry place for 2 months, shaking the jar occasionally.

Strain the ratafia through a non-metallic funnel lined with muslin into a clean, dry bottle. Close the bottle (see pages 12-13). The ratafia is now ready to drink.

Variation: *Satsuma or Tangerine Ratafia*
Substitute satsumas or tangerines for the clementines.

Right: Vin d'Orange and Clementine Ratafia are ideal for drinking on a hot summer's day.

Tangerine and Apple Jam

MAKES ABOUT 1.2KG/2¾LB

600g/1¼lb tangerines
350g/12oz cooking apples
800g/1¾lb warmed sugar (see page 7)
juice of 2 lemons

Halve and chop the tangerines, including the peel, removing and reserving the pips.

Peel, core and slice the apples. Tie the apple cores and peel and the tangerine pips in a muslin bag. Put all the fruit, and peel, and 570ml/1 pint water in a pan, tie the loose end of the muslin bag string on the pan handle so the bag is suspended in the mixture, and bring to the boil, then cover and simmer for 1 hour.

Scoop out the muslin bag with a slotted spoon and press the bag hard with the back of a metal spoon so that the juices run back into the pan.

Over a low heat, stir in the warmed sugar until it has dissolved. Add the lemon juice, raise the heat and boil hard for about 20 minutes, stirring as necessary until setting point is reached (see page 17).

Remove the pan from the heat and skim the scum from the surface with a slotted spoon. Ladle the jam into warm, clean, dry jars. Cover and seal (see pages 12-13). Leave overnight to set slightly. Store in a cool, dark, dry place.

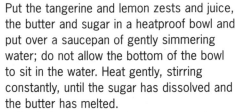

In doughnuts; with apple fritters; added to rhubarb for a crumble, pie or cobbler; spread beneath apple slices in an apple pie; as a filling for warm scones or a roulade.

Tangerine Curd

For extra spice, add grated fresh ginger or lightly crushed cardamom seeds.

MAKES ABOUT 675G/1½LB

finely grated zest and juice of 3 tangerines, about 500g/18oz
finely grated zest and juice of 1 lemon
115g/4oz unsalted butter
300g/10oz caster sugar
4 eggs, size 3, lightly beaten

Put the tangerine and lemon zests and juice, the butter and sugar in a heatproof bowl and put over a saucepan of gently simmering water; do not allow the bottom of the bowl to sit in the water. Heat gently, stirring constantly, until the sugar has dissolved and the butter has melted.

Strain in the eggs and continue to stir over gently simmering water for 30-40 minutes until the curd thickens enough to coat the back of the spoon. Stir occasionally at first but then more frequently as the cooking progresses and constantly towards the end so the curd cooks evenly and does not curdle. The water must not boil.

Pour the curd into warm, clean, dry jars. Cover and seal (see pages 12-13). Store in a cool, dark, dry place or the refrigerator. Refrigerate after opening.

Tangerine Marmalade

Tangerines make a very well-flavoured, clear, fruity marmalade.

MAKES ABOUT 2.7KG/6LB

900g/2lb tangerines
juice of 2 large lemons
1.4kg/3lb warmed sugar (see page 7)

Cut the tangerines in half and squeeze out the juice. Scrape the membranes from the tangerines and tie in a muslin bag with the pips. Cut the peel into thin strips.

Put the tangerine and lemon juices and the peel into a pan with 1.7 litres/3 pints water. Tie the loose end of the muslin bag string on to the pan handle so the bag is suspended in the mixture. Bring to the boil, then simmer for about 1½ hours until the peel is tender and the pan contents have reduced by half.

Scoop out the muslin bag with a slotted

Left (clockwise from front right): kumquats, limes, lemons, clementines and satsumas.

*T*ANGERINES

spoon and press the bag hard with the back of a metal spoon so that the juices flow back into the pan. Discard the bag.

Over a low heat, add the warmed sugar and stir until dissolved. Raise the heat and boil hard for about 15 minutes, stirring if necessary, until setting point is reached (see page 17). Remove from the heat. Skim the scum from the surface with a slotted spoon.

Leave to stand for 10-15 minutes, then stir and ladle into warm, clean, dry jars. Cover and seal (see pages 12-13). Leave overnight. Store in a cool, dark, dry place.

Serve with warm croissants and good coffee for breakfast; use to sandwich the layers of rich chocolate sponge cake.

Tangerine Marmalade Soufflé

Tangerine Marmalade turns inexpensive ingredients into a very special dinner-party dessert.

SERVES 4

2 eggs, size 3, separated
1 egg yolk, size 3
50g/2oz sugar
1½ tablespoons plain flour, sifted
225ml/8fl oz milk
2 tablespoons Tangerine Marmalade
 (see page 70)
2 tablespoons whisky (optional)

Preheat the oven to 200°C/400°F/gas mark 6. Butter four 225ml/8fl oz soufflé dishes.

Whisk together all the egg yolks and the sugar until thick and pale. Gently fold in the sifted flour with a metal spoon.

Bring the milk to the boil in a thick-bottomed saucepan, then slowly pour it into the egg yolk mixture, stirring. Return the mixture to the rinsed saucepan and heat gently, stirring, until thickened; do not allow it to boil. Remove from the heat and stir in the marmalade and whisky, if using.

Whisk the egg whites until stiff but not dry. Stir 2 tablespoons into the marmalade mixture to soften it, then carefully fold in the remainder. Divide between the soufflé dishes. Bake in the centre of the oven for about 13 minutes until well risen and lightly set. Serve immediately.

Left: light, fruity and irresistible, Tangerine Marmalade Soufflé makes the perfect ending to a special meal.

Grapefruit and Apple Curd

MAKES 1-1.5KG/2¼-3¼LB

900g/2lb cooking apples, peeled, cored
 and sliced
225g/8oz unsalted butter, diced
400g/14oz caster sugar
4 eggs, size 3, lightly beaten
grated zest and juice of 1 large grapefruit

Place the apples in a saucepan with a small amount of water, cover the pan and cook gently until the apples are soft and pulpy. Transfer the apples to a heatproof bowl placed over a saucepan of simmering water, and add the butter and sugar. Do not allow the bottom of the bowl to sit in the water. Heat the mixture gently, stirring constantly, until all the sugar has dissolved and the butter has melted.

Strain in the eggs and add the grapefruit zest and juice and continue to stir over gently simmering water until the curd thickens enough to coat the back of the spoon, which can take 30-40 minutes. You need stir only occasionally at first but more frequently as the cooking progresses and constantly towards the end so the curd cooks evenly and does not curdle. The water must not boil.

Pour the curd into warm, clean, dry jars. Cover and seal (see pages 12-13). Store in a cool, dark, dry place or the refrigerator. Refrigerate after opening.

Pink Grapefruit Marmalade

MAKES ABOUT 2.25KG/5LB

2 pink grapefruits
2 lemons
1.8kg/4lb warmed sugar (see page 7)

Cut the fruit in half and squeeze out the juice; set aside the juice and reserve the pips and any membrane that has come away during squeezing and place on a square of muslin. Roughly chop the lemon halves, add to the muslin and then tie into a bag.

Quarter each grapefruit half, then cut across into strips. Put the strips, grapefruit and lemon juices and 2.2 litres/4 pints water into a pan and tie the loose end of string of the muslin bag on to the pan handle so the bag is suspended in the mixture. Bring the mixture to the boil, then simmer for about 45 minutes until the peel is soft.

Remove the muslin bag with a slotted spoon and press the bag hard with the back of a metal spoon so that the juices run back into the pan. Discard the bag.

Over a low heat, stir in the warmed sugar until it has dissolved, then raise the heat and boil hard for 10-15 minutes, stirring as necessary, until setting point is reached (see page 17).

Remove from the heat and skim the scum from the surface with a slotted spoon. Leave to stand for 10-15 minutes, then stir and ladle into warm, clean, dry jars. Cover and seal (see pages 12-13). Leave overnight to set. Store in a cool, dark, dry place.

Kumquats in Vodka and Cointreau

Kumquats are the smallest of the citrus fruits and have a bitter-sweet flavour. Vodka and Cointreau, which is flavoured with bitter and sweet orange peels, go particularly well with kumquats.

MAKES 1.3KG/3LB

175g/6oz sugar
1kg/2¼lb kumquats
300ml/10fl oz vodka
150ml/5fl oz Cointreau

Mix the sugar and 575ml/1 pint water in a saucepan and heat gently, stirring until the sugar dissolves. Meanwhile, prick the kumquats all over with a darning needle. Add them to the pan and simmer for about 15 minutes until the skins feel soft; pierce with a fine skewer to test.

Using a slotted spoon, remove the kumquats from the syrup and pack into warm, clean, dry jars. Pour the vodka and Cointreau over the kumquats, then top up with the reserved syrup.

Cover and seal the jars (see pages 12-13). Invert them gently to mix the liquids. Store in a cool, dark, dry place for at least 1 month before eating.

⸺⸺

Serve with crème fraîche, Greek yogurt, creamy rice pudding, steamed ginger pudding or slices of gingerbread.

Pickled Kumquats with Cardamom

Kumquats are unlike other citrus fruits, since the peel is sweeter than the flesh. They produce an excellent tart-sweetness especially if combined with honey and spices.

MAKES 675G/1½LB

500g/18oz kumquats
1 teaspoon sea salt
200ml/7fl oz white wine vinegar
4 tablespoons clear honey
3 cardamom pods, crushed
1 clove
1.25cm/½in piece of fresh ginger,
 thinly sliced then cut into fine shreds

Cut the kumquats in half, then put them in a saucepan with the salt and water to cover. Bring to the boil then simmer for 5 minutes. Drain the kumquats, discarding any pips.

$\mathcal{K}$ UMQUATS

Put the vinegar, honey, cardamom pods, clove and ginger into a pan and heat gently, stirring, until the honey has dissolved. Raise the heat and bring to the boil, then add the kumquats.

Ladle the kumquats and the liquid into warm, clean, dry jars. Cover with vinegar-proof lids and seal (see pages 12-13). Store in a cool, dark, dry place for 1 month before eating.

Serve with duck or game terrines; add a generous spoonful to the cooking juices of roast duck or pork.

Kumquat Conserve

This is fruity, sharp and sweet with a little 'kick' of whisky.

MAKES ABOUT 1.4KG/3LB

675g/1½lb ripe kumquats
675g/1½lb sugar
4 tablespoons whisky

Using a sharp knife, chop the kumquats into coarse chunks and then layer them with the sugar in a bowl. Cover and leave in a cool place for 1 day.

Tip the contents of the bowl into a saucepan, add 300ml/10fl oz water and heat gently, stirring, until the sugar has dissolved. Raise the heat and boil rapidly for 10 minutes until the liquid is syrupy.

Remove from the heat, stir in the whisky and leave to stand for 10-15 minutes. Stir, then ladle into warm, clean, dry jars. Cover and seal (see pages 12-13). Leave overnight to set. Store in a cool, dark, dry place.

Right: Lime Shred Marmalade and Kumquat Conserve make a deliciously tangy addition to the breakfast table.

Chicken Tagine with Preserved Lemons and Olives

Preserved lemons are used in many Moroccan dishes but this is one of the best known. The mellow flavour of the preserved lemons is beautifully complemented by pinky-brown Moroccan olives; if you cannot find these, substitute Greek Kalamata olives.

SERVES 4

1 Spanish onion, finely chopped
2-3 tablespoons olive oil
3 garlic cloves, chopped
salt and freshly ground black pepper
¾ teaspoon ground ginger
1 teaspoon ground cinnamon
large pinch of saffron threads, toasted
 and crushed
1 chicken, weighing about 1.6kg/3½lb
700ml/1¼ pints chicken stock or water
115g/4oz pinky-brown Moroccan olives, rinsed
1 Moroccan Preserved Lemon (see page 75),
 discard flesh if liked, rinsed and chopped
large bunch of fresh coriander, finely chopped
large bunch of fresh parsley, finely chopped

Gently fry the onion in the oil, stirring frequently, until it is softened and a good golden colour.

Meanwhile, crush the garlic with a pinch of salt, then work in the ginger, cinnamon, saffron and a little pepper. Stir into the onions and continue cooking until fragrant.

Put the chicken in a heavy-based saucepan or flameproof casserole that it just fits, spread the onion mixture all over, then add the stock or water and bring to just on simmering point. Cover and simmer very gently for about 1¼ hours, turning the chicken over 2 or 3 times.

Right: Chicken Tagine with Preserved Lemons and Olives makes an exotic supper dish.

ℒEMONS

Add the olives, preserved lemon, coriander and parsley, cover again and cook for a further 15 minutes or so until the chicken is very tender.

Taste the sauce – if the flavour needs to be more concentrated, transfer the chicken to a warm, shallow serving dish, cover and keep warm, then boil the cooking juices to reduce them to a rich sauce. Tilt the pan and skim off the surplus fat, if liked, then pour the sauce over the chicken.

Moroccan Preserved Lemons

Lemons lose their sharpness when preserved in salt. The unique flavour and silken texture that develops when you use this technique is a characteristic of North African, and especially Moroccan, cooking. Yet the lemons also make a novel addition to non-Moroccan dishes. You will find that these lemons are easy to prepare, and thin-skinned lemons yield the most juice. Traditionally, only the peel of the preserved fruit is used, but I usually include the flesh as well.

Once the jar has been opened, the fruit will keep for up to 1 year unrefrigerated (do not worry if a lacy white film appears on top of the jar or on the lemons as it is quite harmless – simply rinse it off); a layer of olive oil floated on the surface will help to preserve freshness.

7 tablespoons sea salt
7 plump, juicy lemons, preferably thin-skinned

Put 1 teaspoon coarse salt in the bottom of a clean, dry jar. Holding a lemon over a plate to catch the juice, cut lengthways 4 times as if about to quarter it, but do not cut quite through – leave the pieces joined. Ease out any pips. Pack 1 tablespoon salt into the cuts, then close them up around the salt

and put the lemon in the jar. Repeat with 5 more fruit, packing them tightly and pressing each layer down hard to expel any air before adding the next layer, until the jar is full.

Squeeze another lemon and pour the juice over the fruit. Sprinkle with more coarse salt and top up with boiling water to cover the fruit. Close the jar tightly and keep in a warmish place for 3-4 weeks before using.

In spicy lamb, chicken and fish casseroles; use the juice in salad dressings.

Lemon and Passionfruit Curd

This delectable spread combines the sharp, clean taste of lemon with scented passionfruit.

MAKES ABOUT 450G/1LB

1 teaspoon finely grated lemon zest
115ml/4fl oz lemon juice (about 2½ lemons)
75g/3oz unsalted butter, diced
225g/8oz caster sugar
3 eggs, size 2 or 3, lightly beaten
2 passionfruit, halved and pulp scooped out

Put the lemon zest and juice, butter and sugar in a heatproof bowl and put over a saucepan of gently simmering water; do not allow the base of the bowl to sit in the water. Heat gently, stirring constantly, until the sugar has dissolved and the butter melted.

Strain in the eggs and continue to stir over gently simmering water until the curd thickens enough to coat the back of the spoon, which can take 30-40 minutes. You need stir only occasionally at first but more frequently as the cooking progresses and constantly towards the end so the curd cooks evenly and does not curdle. The water must not boil.

Remove the bowl from the heat and stir in the passionfruit pulp. Pour the curd into warm, clean, dry jars. Cover and seal (see pages 12-13). Store in a cool, dark, dry place or the refrigerator. Refrigerate after opening.

Diluted with extra lemon juice and some rum, white or dark, this makes a superb sauce for spooning over a cheesecake.

St Clement's Cordial

Mixtures of orange and lemon are often called St Clement's after the nursery rhyme, *The Bells of St Clement's*. If you prefer a smooth drink, strain the cordial through a non-metallic sieve lined with a double thickness of muslin; squeeze the pulp in the muslin in order to extract the maximum amount of juice.

MAKES ABOUT 1.3 LITRES/2¼ PINTS

about 6 large juicy oranges
about 3 lemons
675g/1½lb sugar

Grate the zest from 1½ oranges and 1½ lemons. Squeeze the juice from all the oranges to make about 550ml/19fl oz juice, and all the lemons to make about 250ml/ 9fl oz.

Put the fruit juices and zests into a saucepan, add the sugar and heat gently, stirring, until the sugar has dissolved. Raise the heat slightly and bring to just below boiling point.

Immediately remove the pan from the heat and pour the cordial into warm, clean, dry bottles. Cover and process in a waterbath (see page 13). Alternatively, leave the cordial to cool, then pour it into cold bottles and keep in the refrigerator for up to 1 month.

Lime Curd

Use limes in place of lemons to make a fruity, tangy change to the more traditional lemon curd (for lemon curd recipe, see variation below).

MAKES ABOUT 675G/1½LB

finely grated zest and juice of 5 large, juicy limes
115g/4oz unsalted butter, diced
300g/10oz caster sugar
4 eggs, size 3, lightly beaten

Put the lime zest and juice, butter and sugar in a heatproof bowl and put over a saucepan of gently simmering water; do not allow the bottom of the bowl to sit in the water. Heat the mixture gently, stirring constantly, until all the sugar has dissolved and the butter has melted.

Strain the eggs into the bowl and continue to stir over gently simmering water until the curd thickens enough to coat the back of the spoon. This should take about 30-40 minutes. You need stir only occasionally at first but more frequently as the cooking progresses, then constantly towards the end of the cooking time so the curd cooks evenly and does not curdle. Do not allow the water to boil.

Pour the curd into warm, clean, dry jars. Cover and seal (see pages 12-13). Store in a cool dark, dry place or the refrigerator. Refrigerate after opening.

Variation: *Lemon Curd*
Use 4 medium, plump lemons in place of the limes. Follow the recipe above. Makes about 675g/1½lb.

Lime Shred Marmalade

My grandmother had a particular passion for Lime Shred Marmalade. She would spread it very thickly on her breakfast toast and have it in sandwiches for tea (white bread had to be bought specially – this marmalade goes better with white bread than brown). I used to make her a batch for her birthday and for Christmas. One year, as a special treat, I used the peel from Thai kaffir limes. The marmalade was eaten with even greater relish, so from then on I always used kaffir lime peel (the rest of the fruit is never used).

MAKES ABOUT 2.2KG/5LB

675g/1½lb limes (about 12) *or* **675g/1½lb limes (for flesh only) and 450g/1lb kaffir limes (for peel only)**
1.4kg/3lb warmed sugar (see page 7)

Peel the limes thinly, then cut the peel into thin strips. Thinly slice the flesh, reserving any juice, and tie the pips into a muslin bag.

Put the fruit, any reserved juice, the peel and 1.6 litres/2¾ pints water into a pan and tie the loose end of string on to the pan handle so the bag is suspended in the mixture. Simmer for about 1 hour until the peel is tender and the contents of the pan reduced by about half.

Scoop out the muslin bag with a slotted spoon and, wearing rubber gloves to protect your hands from the hot liquid, squeeze hard to press the juices back into the pan. Discard the muslin bag.

Over a low heat, stir in the warmed sugar until it has dissolved. Raise the heat and boil hard for 10-15 minutes, stirring as necessary, until setting point is reached (see page 17).

Remove from the heat and skim off any scum from the surface with a slotted spoon. Leave to stand for 10-15 minutes, then stir and ladle into warm, clean, dry jars. Cover and seal (see pages 12-13). Leave over-night. Store in a cool, dark, dry place.

Variation: *Lemon Shred Marmalade*
Substitute the same weight of lemons for the limes. Makes about 2.2kg/5lb.

Lime Chutney

If you can resist dipping into this pungent chutney, it is best to keep it for up to 1 year before eating to allow the flavours to develop.

MAKES ABOUT 2.2KG/5LB

900g/2lb large limes, thinly sliced
450g/1lb onions, finely chopped
25g/1oz sea salt
7g/¼oz coriander seeds
15g/½oz allspice berries
7g/¼oz whole cardamon pods, crushed
4 dried red chillies, seeded, if liked, and chopped
50g/2oz fresh ginger, grated
570ml/1 pint white wine vinegar
450g/1lb warmed caster sugar (see page 7)

Put the limes, onions and salt in a large non-metallic bowl. Place the coriander seeds, allspice berries and cardamom pods on a square of muslin and tie together with string to make a bag. Stir the bag into the bowl. Cover the bowl and leave in a cool place for 1 day.

Tip the contents of the bowl into a saucepan and stir in the chillies, ginger and vinegar. Bring the mixture to the boil, then lower the heat and simmer for 1½ hours, stirring occasionally.

Add the warmed sugar to the saucepan and stir until all the sugar has dissolved. Raise the heat and bring to the boil, then lower the heat and simmer, stirring occasionally, until the chutney is thick and there is no free liquid. Scoop out the muslin bag and discard. Ladle the chutney into warm, clean, dry jars, taking care not to trap any air bubbles. Cover with vinegar-proof lids

*L*IMES

and seal (see pages 12-13). Store in a cool, dark, dry place for at least 1 month, or up to 1 year, before eating (see above).

Serve this chutney with curries and other spicy dishes.

Indian Sweet-sour Lime Pickle

Long pickling causes lime wedges to turn almost gelatinous and gives them a wonderful flavour. Fresh mint goes very well with lime and ginger, so I sometimes include a few leaves in the pickle and then halve the amount of garlic.

MAKES ABOUT 850ML/1½ PINTS

12-14 limes
7.5cm/3in piece of fresh ginger, peeled, thinly
 sliced and then cut into fine strips
4 garlic cloves, quartered lengthways (optional)
6 teaspoons sea salt
about 3 fresh green chillies
225ml/8fl oz white wine vinegar
400g/14oz sugar

Cut 6 limes lengthways into 6 wedges each. Put a layer of lime wedges in the bottom of a wide-necked jar, with their cut sides facing outwards. Sprinkle with some of the ginger and some of the garlic, if used, and about 1 teaspoon of the salt. Repeat the layering, pressing down on the ingredients slightly to expel air, and adding a chilli here and there, until the jar is full to within 1.25-2cm/½-¾in from the top.

Squeeze the juice from the remaining limes to make 200ml/7fl oz. Pour into a saucepan with the vinegar and sugar and heat gently, stirring, until the sugar has dissolved, then simmer gently until the mixture becomes lightly syrupy.

Pour the mixture into the jar and swivel the jar to expel any air bubbles. If the top layer of limes floats to the surface, weight them down with a pad of greaseproof paper. Cover the jar with a vinegar-proof lid and seal (see pages 12-13).

Leave in a sunny or warm place for 1 month, then store for another 2-4 weeks at room temperature before eating.

Serve with tandoori chicken, Indian spinach dishes, or to accompany salmon; use as a filling in cheese sandwiches.

Above: Indian Sweet-sour Lime Pickle makes an attractive and zesty accompaniment to a whole range of spicy dishes.

$\mathcal{S}$OFT $\mathcal{F}$RUITS

*Soft fruits have always been prime candidates
for preserving as they traditionally
have limited growing seasons.
However, by using
genetics and selection,
growers have extended
natural seasons, but the
quantities are small, the price
high and the flavour disappointingly mild.
(Flavour is not just a question of exposure to sun, but
also of comparatively slow ripening.) As far as I am
concerned, soft fruits still remain a seasonal crop. Some
of the most popular, as well as the most innovative of
preserves can be made from soft fruit: in this chapter you
will find preserves ranging from traditional Blackberry
Jam (see page 80), to Spiced Cranberry and Apple
Sauce (see page 85), and Red Summer Fruits Preserve
(see page 91). When preparing soft fruits for cooking,
handle them gently and, unless they are very dirty,
do not rinse them in water. If they are slightly soiled,
wipe them carefully with a damp cloth, otherwise
it is best to keep them dry.*

*Left (from left to right): Strawberry Conserve, Blackberry Jam, Red
Summer Fruits Preserve and Superlative Redcurrant Jelly.*

Auvergnat Conserved Bilberries

When researching a book on the food along the river Loire, I found this recipe in an old book of Auvergnat recipes I bought near Le Puy food market. The result looks like bottled bilberries, but tastes fresher.

bilberries
sugar
lemon juice

Preheat the oven to its lowest setting.

Weigh the berries and reserve some for topping up the jars later.

Pack the remaining bilberries firmly into clean, dry jars (use 500ml/18fl oz jars, if you have them), sprinkling in about 1 tablespoon lemon juice and 85g/3oz sugar for every 450g/1lb fruit. Put the reserved berries in a jar.

Put all the jars of fruit on the bottom shelf of the oven for 45-50 minutes until the jars are thoroughly hot. The fruit will have shrunk a little so top up the jar with the reserved berries. Pour boiling water into the jars to cover the fruit completely and seal immediately. Leave overnight before eating. Store in a cool, dark, dry place.

Serve over ice cream or plain sponge cake and accompany with cream; serve with pancakes or drop scones.

Blackberry Jam

Recipes always used to specify using unripe blackberries to get a good set, but now, with sugar with pectin so readily available, this is not vital. The flavour and juiciness of the berries is of greater importance. The length of time you will need to cook the fruit,

if, indeed, you need to cook it at all, will depend very much on the blackberries; reduce the water in relation to the reduction in the cooking time.

MAKES ABOUT 1.6KG/3½LB

1kg/2¼lb blackberries
juice of ½ lemon
1kg/2¼lb warmed sugar with pectin (see page 7)
2 tablespoons gin (optional)

Put the blackberries, lemon juice and 4 tablespoons water in a pan, cover and heat very gently, shaking the pan occasionally, for 10-15 minutes until the fruit is soft.

Carefully stir in the sugar over a low heat, taking care not to break up the berries, until it is dissolved. Raise the heat and boil hard for about 4 minutes or until setting point is reached (see page 17).

Remove from the heat and stir in the gin, if using. Ladle into warm, clean, dry jars. Cover and seal (see pages 12-13). Leave overnight. Store in a cool, dark, dry place.

Variation: *Raspberry Jam*
Use 900g/2lb each raspberries and sugar with pectin, and the juice of 1 lemon. Gently heat all the ingredients, stirring carefully, until the sugar has dissolved. Proceed with the recipe above. Makes about 1.8kg/4lb.

Blackberry Cheese

According to an old saying you should pick blackberries before the end of September, when the devil spits on them. If he does, he didn't spoil the wonderful dark colour or rich flavour of the cheese I made last year.

MAKES ABOUT 1.4KG/3LB

1.4kg/3lb blackberries
1 tablespoon lemon juice
warmed sugar (see page 7)

Put the blackberries and lemon juice in a pan, add barely enough water to cover and bring to the boil, then simmer for about 15 minutes until the fruit is soft and pulpy.

Press the fruit through a non-metallic sieve. Measure the purée and return it to the rinsed pan. Add 350g/12oz sugar for 570ml/1 pint purée and heat gently, stirring, until the sugar has dissolved. Raise the heat and boil gently, stirring frequently, for 45-55 minutes until the mixture is so thick that when the spoon is drawn across the bottom of the pan, a clear trail is left.

Spoon into warm, clean, dry jars, or into lightly oiled decorative moulds, taking care not to trap any air bubbles. Cover and seal (see pages 12-13). Store in a cool, dark, dry place for 2-3 months before eating.

This is an excellent accompaniment to mature Cheddar cheese, crusty, firm-textured white bread and unsalted butter.

Blackberry Cordial

This is an old-fashioned sharp/sweet cordial. Blackberries should be large, ripe and glossy, so, pass over any small, hard pippy fruit – they really aren't worth bothering with.

MAKES AT LEAST 1.9 LITRES/3½ PINTS

900g/2lb blackberries
570ml/1 pint white wine vinegar
450g/1lb sugar
225g/8oz clear honey

Put the fruit and vinegar in a non-metallic bowl. Crush the fruit with a wooden spoon, then cover the bowl and leave in a cool place for 1 week, stirring and pressing the fruit 2 or 3 times a day.

Strain the contents of the bowl through a non-metallic sieve into a pan, pressing hard on the sieve with the wooden spoon to

ℬLACKBERRIES

extract as much juice as possible. Stir in the sugar and honey and heat gently until the sugar has dissolved. Raise the heat and boil for 5 minutes, stirring as necessary.

Pour the cordial into warm, clean, dry bottles and leave to cool, then cover and seal (see pages 12-13). Store in a cool, dark, dry place.

———— ✐ ————

Add 1 tablespoonful to a mug of hot water as a soothing cough and cold reliever, or as a pleasant drink at bedtime or on a cold day.

Below: the combination of blackberries and elderberries produces this fruity Hedgerow Jelly.

Hedgerow Jelly

Long but gentle cooking produces this fruity-flavoured jelly. For blackberry jelly, substitute blackberries for the elderberries.

MAKES 1.1LITRES/2½LB

3 large lemons
generous 2.7kg/6lb blackberries and
 elderberries
warmed sugar

Squeeze the juice from the lemons and reserve the pips. Put the juice, pips, berries and 6 tablespoons water in a heavy casserole and stir together. Lay greaseproof paper on the fruit, then cover the casserole.

Cook in a very low oven for a few hours (overnight in the bottom of an Aga is ideal) until the fruit is meltingly tender.

Crush the fruit with a potato masher, then tip the contents of the casserole into a scalded jelly bag suspended over a non-metallic bowl and leave to strain, undisturbed, in a cool place for 8-12 hours.

Measure the juice and put into a pan with 450g/1lb sugar for every 570ml/1 pint juice. Heat gently, stirring, until the sugar has dissolved, then raise the heat and boil hard for about 15 minutes until setting point is reached (see page 17). Immediately ladle into warm, clean, dry jars. Cover and seal (see pages 12-13). Leave overnight to set. Store in a cool, dark, dry place.

Duck Salad with Blackberry Dressing

Stirred into the cooking juices from the duck, Quick Savoury Blackberry Jelly makes a lightly spiced dressing for a warm salad.

SERVES 4

Four 150-175g/5-6oz duck breasts
sea salt and freshly ground black pepper
mixed salad leaves, such as watercress, rocket,
 lamb's lettuce, baby spinach, curly endive and
 oak leaf lettuce
flat-leaf parsley
1½ tablespoons red wine
1 tablespoon red wine vinegar
1 tablespoon Quick Savoury Blackberry Jelly
 (see right)
about 1½ tablespoons sunflower seeds

Heat the oven to 230°C/450°F/gas mark 8.
   Rub the duck breasts with salt, then score the skin with the point of a sharp knife. Put the breasts, skin side up, on a rack in a roasting tin and roast for 15 minutes.
   Divide the salad leaves and parsley between 4 plates.
   Transfer the duck to a warm plate and keep warm for about 10 minutes.
   Tilt the roasting tin and spoon off the surplus fat, leaving behind the juices. Put the tin on the hob to caramelize the juices. Stir in the wine and vinegar to dislodge the sediment and bring to the boil for 1-2 minutes, stirring frequently.
   Remove from the heat and stir in the jelly, then set aside. Cut the duck into strips and add them to the salad leaves and sprinkle with the sunflower seeds.
   Gently reheat the sauce in the roasting tin to dissolve the jelly, then bring to the boil. Pour over the duck and salad leaves, toss lightly and serve.

Right: Quick Savoury Blackberry Jelly makes a delicious dressing for this sweet-sour Duck Salad.

Quick Savoury Blackberry Jelly

Simple straining through an ordinary non-metallic sieve instead of lengthy straining through a jelly bag is all that is needed to produce this magnificent dark, firm, richly flavoured jelly. If serving it as an accompaniment, present it on a white plate or in a white bowl to show off its deep colour.

MAKES ABOUT 1.4KG/3LB

1 tablespoon cloves
2 cinnamon sticks
1 teaspoon allspice berries
1.8kg/4lb blackberries
150ml/5fl oz Spiced Vinegar (see page 139)
900g/2lb warmed sugar (see page 7)

Tie the cloves, cinnamon sticks and allspice berries in a muslin bag and put in a saucepan together with the blackberries and vinegar. Bring the mixture to the boil,

$\mathscr{B}$LACKBERRIES, $\mathscr{B}$LUEBERRIES

then simmer gently, stirring occasionally, for about 30 minutes.

Strain the mixture through a non-metallic sieve and return to the pan. Discard the bag. Over a low heat, stir in the warmed sugar until it has dissolved, then continue to simmer, stirring as necessary, until well thickened.

Ladle the jelly into warm, clean, dry jars or pots. Cover and seal (see pages 12-13). Store in a cool, dark, dry place for at least 3 weeks before eating.

Serve with game, pork, turkey or duck, or add to casseroles made with them.

Blackberry and Apple Jelly with Thyme

You can vary the amount of thyme used in this recipe according to taste.

MAKES 1.4KG/3LB

675g/1½lb cooking apples, preferably Bramleys
1.4kg/3lb blackberries
handful of thyme sprigs
warmed sugar (see page 7)
thyme leaves (optional)

Coarsely chop the apples without peeling or coring them, then put them into a pan with the blackberries, thyme sprigs and 850ml/ 1 pint water. Bring to the boil, then simmer for 1 hour, stirring occasionally, until the fruit is soft.

Tip the contents of the pan into a scalded jelly bag suspended over a non-metallic bowl and leave to strain, undisturbed, in a cool place for 8-12 hours.

Measure the strained juice and put into a pan with 450g/1lb warmed sugar for every 570ml/1 pint juice. Heat gently, stirring, until the sugar has dissolved, then raise the heat

and boil hard for about 15 minutes until setting point is reached (see page 17).

Remove the pan from the heat and taste a little of the jelly – if the thyme flavour is not strong enough, leave to stand for 10-15 minutes, then stir in some thyme leaves. Ladle into warm, clean, dry jars. Cover and seal (see pages 12-13). Leave overnight to set. Store in a cool, dark, dry place.

Blueberry Curd

With their sweet, spicy juiciness blueberries are ideal candidates for making a fruit curd.

MAKES 450G/1LB

225g/8oz blueberries
50g/2oz unsalted butter, diced
225g/8oz caster sugar
3 eggs, size 3, lightly beaten

Place the blueberries in a covered saucepan with 1 tablespoon water and cook gently, shaking the pan occasionally, until very soft (about 10 minutes). Press through a fine non-metallic sieve into a heatproof non-metallic bowl, then stir in the butter and sugar and put over a saucepan of gently simmering water; do not allow the bottom of the bowl to sit in the water. Heat gently, stirring, until the sugar has dissolved and the butter has melted.

Strain in the eggs and continue to stir over gently simmering water until the curd thickens enough to coat the back of the spoon, which should take 30-40 minutes. You need stir only occasionally at first but more frequently as the cooking progresses, then constantly towards the end so the curd cooks evenly and does not curdle. The water must not boil.

Strain the curd into warm, clean, dry jars. Cover and seal (see pages 12-13). Store in a cold, dark, dry place or the refrigerator. Refrigerate after opening.

Blueberry Jam

Bay leaves enhance the sweet, spicy flavour of blueberries.

MAKES ABOUT 1.6KG/3½LB

1.4kg/3lb blueberries
juice of 2 lemons
4 small fresh bay leaves
1kg/2¼lb sugar with pectin

Stir the blueberries, lemon juice, bay leaves and half the sugar together in a non-metallic bowl, crushing the berries slightly. Cover and leave in a cool place for 6-8 hours.

Tip the contents of the bowl into a pan, add the remaining sugar and stir over a low heat until the sugar has dissolved. Raise the heat and boil hard for 4 minutes until setting point is reached (see page 17).

Remove from the heat, scoop out the bay leaves and skim off any scum. Leave to stand for 10-15 minutes. Stir gently, then pour into warm, clean, dry jars. Cover and seal (see pages 12-13). Leave overnight to set. Store in a cool, dark, dry place.

Below: blueberries belong to the same genus of plants as bilberries and cranberries.

Cranberry Chutney

Bright red cranberries are too sour to eat raw but, once cooked, they can be transformed into a variety of delicious sauces and chutneys. This is a cleaner, lighter chutney than many; I prefer to use white rather than brown sugar, as it keeps the colour and flavour light.

MAKES ABOUT 1.1KG/2½LB

450g/1lb cranberries
450g/1lb dessert apples, peeled, cored and chopped
115g/4oz raisins
25g/1oz fresh ginger, peeled and grated
grated zest of 1 orange
½ cinnamon stick
pinch of ground cloves
rock or sea salt
about 275g/9oz white sugar
425ml/15fl oz white wine or cider vinegar

Put all the ingredients into a pan and heat gently, stirring, until the sugar has dissolved. Raise the heat and bring the contents of the pan to the boil, then simmer gently for about 30 minutes, stirring occasionally, until all the fruit is soft and the chutney is quite thick and there is no free liquid.

Spoon the chutney into warm, clean, dry jars making sure that you do not trap any air bubbles. Cover the chutney with vinegar-proof lids and seal (see pages 12-13). Store in a cool, dark, dry place for at least 2 months before eating.

Left: Cranberry Chutney goes particularly well with good, fresh bread and a variety of traditional hard cheeses.

CRANBERRIES

Spiced Cranberry and Apple Sauce

Traditional pickling spices, sharp fruit, vinegar and sugar combine to make an appealing fruity, sharp and sweet sauce that is good with pork or hot or cold duck.

MAKES ABOUT 900G/2LB

450g/1lb cranberries
225g/8oz cooking apples, preferably Bramleys, peeled, cored (see page 56) and chopped
300ml/10fl oz white wine vinegar
6 cloves
6 allspice berries
2 blades of mace
2 cinnamon sticks
350g/12oz warmed sugar (see page 7)

Put the cranberries, apples and vinegar into a pan. Put the spices on a square of muslin and tie into a bag with a long length of string. Tie the free end of the string to the handle of the pan so the bag is resting on the fruit. Bring to the boil, then cover and simmer for 10 minutes until the cranberries and apples are soft but retain their shape.

Remove the pan from the heat and stir in the warmed sugar. Heat gently, stirring, until

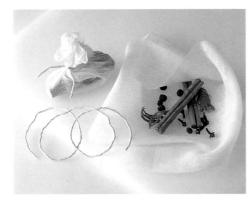

Preserving with spices: tie spices in a piece of muslin or cheesecloth. The spices will flavour the preserve and the bag is easy to remove.

the sugar has dissolved, then simmer for about 20 minutes until thickened.

Discard the spice bag and pour the sauce into warm, clean, dry jars. Cover with vinegar-proof lids and seal (see pages 12-13). Store in a cool, dark, dry place for 6-8 weeks before eating.

Quick Cranberry and Orange Jelly

This recipe is a jelly because it does not contain any pieces of fruit or pips, yet it does not have the usual clarity of jellies. As the cooked fruit is pressed through a sieve, rather than left to strain for hours, the whole process is a much quicker one. Needless to say, this jelly goes well with Thanksgiving or Christmas roast turkey, served hot or cold. It also finds a home in many sweet dishes.

MAKES ABOUT 900G/2LB

450g/1lb cranberries
grated zest of 1 orange
450g/1lb warmed sugar (see page 7)

Put the cranberries, orange zest and 300ml/10fl oz water in a pan and bring to the boil over a moderate heat, then simmer, stirring occasionally, for 10 minutes until the cranberries pop and the mixture becomes a thick pulp.

Press the contents of the pan through a non-metallic sieve.

Return the purée to the rinsed pan and add the warmed sugar. Heat gently, stirring, until the sugar has dissolved, then heat for about 5 minutes until small bubbles just begin to appear around the edge of the pan.

Remove from the heat immediately and ladle into warm clean, dry jars. Cover and seal (see pages 12-13). Leave overnight to set. Store in a cool, dark, dry place.

Cranberry Ketchup

Cranberry Ketchup makes a more than acceptable alternative to cranberry jelly with turkey.

MAKES ABOUT 570-850ML/1-1½ PINTS

900g/2lb cranberries
225g/8oz onions, chopped
150ml/5fl oz white wine vinegar
300g/10oz sugar
1 teaspoon salt
6 allspice berries
4 cloves
10 black peppercorns
5cm/2in piece cinnamon stick

Put the cranberries, onions and 300ml/ 10fl oz water in a pan and bring to the boil, then simmer gently until the cranberries have burst and the onion is tender. Pass through the fine disc of a vegetable mill or a fine non-metallic sieve.

Return the purée to the rinsed pan with the vinegar, sugar and salt. Tie the spices in a square of muslin and add to the pan. Heat gently, stirring until the sugar has dissolved. Raise the heat and bring to the boil, then simmer for about 15 minutes until the sauce has the consistency of thick double cream and there is no free moisture.

Discard the spice bag and pour the ketchup into warm, clean, dry bottles. Cover and seal (see pages 12-13). Store in a cool, dark, dry place for 2-3 weeks before eating.

Cranberry Ketchup is useful to have in reserve, as a couple of spoonfuls can be stirred into the cooking juices of turkey steaks or sausages to make a quick gravy. It is also excellent for livening up many sauces and casseroles.

Crisp Loganberry and Pear Filo Rolls

The sharpness of loganberries teams well with the soft flavour of pears in this modern, light, quick-and-easy version of strudel.

SERVES 4

**4 generous tablespoons Loganberry Jam
 (see right)
40g/1½oz raisins
50g/2oz fresh breadcrumbs
1 teaspoon ground cinnamon
1 large pear, peeled, cored and quartered
4 sheets of filo pastry
melted unsalted butter for brushing
sifted icing sugar for dusting**

Preheat the oven to 180°C/350°F/gas mark 4. Lightly butter a baking sheet.

Mix together the loganberry jam, raisins, breadcrumbs and cinnamon.

Brush one sheet of filo pastry with melted butter, then fold it in half and brush again with butter. Spoon a quarter of the cranberry mixture along the edge nearest you and put a pear quarter on top. Fold the sides of the pastry over the filling then roll up neatly. Transfer to the baking sheet, putting the seam side down. Repeat with the remaining filling, pastry and pear quarters.

Brush each roll with melted butter and bake for 20-30 minutes until pale golden. Serve hot or cold dusted with icing sugar.

Right: Crisp Loganberry and Pear Filo Rolls consist of individual plump cushions of fruit wrapped in a crunchy layer of pastry.

Loganberry Jam

For as long as I can remember, loganberries have been grown by my family, first by my grandparents and then by my mother. They always seem to have been planted so the berries are difficult to reach, but that, and the sharp prickles, never deterred even small hands and arms from reaching for the plump, sweet fruit. Loganberries are particularly flavoursome berries.

MAKES ABOUT 2.15KG/4¾LB

**1.4kg/3lb loganberries
juice of ½ lemon
1.4kg/3lb warmed sugar (see page 7)**

Gently heat the loganberries and lemon juice in a covered heavy casserole in a very low oven until soft and thoroughly hot (45-60 minutes). Alternatively, gently heat the fruit and lemon juice in a pan without any water until the juice runs, then simmer for about 15 minutes, stirring carefully occasionally, until the fruit is very soft.

Tip the contents of the casserole into a pan. Over a low heat, gently stir in the sugar until it has dissolved. Raise the heat and boil hard for about 10 minutes until setting point is reached (see page 17).

Remove from the heat and skim the scum from the surface with a slotted spoon. Leave to stand for 10-15 minutes. Stir and ladle into warm, clean, dry jars. Cover and seal (see pages 12-13). Leave overnight to set. Store in a cool, dark, dry place.

Quick Uncooked Raspberry Jam

To gain the full benefit of this jam, which preserves the true fresh flavour of the fruit, use the most full-flavoured berries you can find. The taste of raspberries that do not quite reach this ideal can be boosted with *eau-de-vie de framboise* (raspberry *eau-de-vie*). Instead of adding kirsch to the fruit mixture, try flavouring the jam with rose water. The jam is much softer than conventionally boiled jams.

MAKES ABOUT 900G/2LB

450g/1lb raspberries
450g/1lb caster sugar
1 tablespoon kirsch (optional)

Preheat the oven to 170°C/325°F/gas mark 3. Put the raspberries and sugar in separate large heat-proof bowls, cover and put in the oven for 20-30 minutes until very hot but not quite boiling.

Tip the raspberries and caster sugar into a large bowl and stir together thoroughly using a wooden spoon. Stir in the kirsch, if using, then spoon into warm, clean, dry jars. Cover and seal (see pages 12-13). Store in a cool, dark, dry place for at least 1 month before eating.

Serve over peaches, strawberries or pears or eat with fresh unsalted cream cheese, fromage frais or mascarpone cheese. Crisp almond biscuits make a good companion to any of these.

Framboise

When 'genuine' French liqueurs such as framboise and cassis are made, the fruit is macerated in molasses spirits for about 2 months before the juice is squeezed out, sweetened and distilled. This is a much easier method, but the result is still delicious, both as a drink or with desserts.

MAKES 1.1 LITRES/2 PINTS

450g/1lb raspberries
570ml/1 pint brandy
about 350g/12oz sugar

Lightly crush the raspberries, then put them in a screw-top jar with the brandy. Close tightly and leave in a cool, dark, dry place for 2 months.

Strain the liqueur through a non-metallic sieve lined with muslin, measure the liquid and stir in 175g/6oz sugar for every 570ml/1 pint. Cover and leave for 2 days, stirring occasionally to dissolve the sugar.

Pour the framboise into bottles, seal (see pages 12-13) and store in a cool, dark, dry place for at least 6 months before drinking.

Variations: *Crème de Cassis*
Follow the recipe above, simply substituting blackcurrants for raspberries. Makes about 1.1 litres/2 pints.
Crème de Mûres
Follow the recipe above, simply substituting blackberries for raspberries. Makes about 1.1 litres/2 pints.

Dilute with still or sparkling dry white wine; pour over fruit such as peaches, strawberries or pears; pour over creamy desserts and ice cream.

Below (from left to right): fresh loganberries and raspberries.

Strawberry Conserve

Making this preserve, which captures the true, fresh flavour of strawberries and contains whole plump berries, doesn't take much time although the method does stretch over 3 days.

MAKES ABOUT 1.4KG/3LB

1kg/2¼lb strawberries, hulled
900g/2lb warmed sugar (see page 7)
juice of 1 lemon or orange

Layer the strawberries and warmed sugar in a pan, cover and leave overnight in a cool place, by which time most of the sugar should have dissolved.

Gently heat the pan to dissolve any remaining sugar and draw the juice from the fruit; give an occasional gentle stir or shake the pan so the fruit stays whole. Add the lemon or orange juice, raise the heat and boil for 5 minutes.

Carefully pour the mixture into a non-metallic bowl, cover and leave in a cool place for 2 days. Return to the pan, bring to the boil and boil hard for 10 minutes. Remove from the heat and skim any scum from the surface with a slotted spoon. Leave to stand for 10-15 minutes. Stir and ladle into warm, clean, dry jars. Cover and seal (see pages 12-13). Leave overnight to set. Store in a cool, dark, dry place.

Freezer Strawberry Jam

Freezer jams have a very soft set. If you use sugar with pectin, as in this recipe, or add liquid pectin, you will have a firmer set. Use containers that will neither react with the acid in the fruit nor crack when frozen. Freezer jams can be frozen for up to 6 months. Once thawed they must be kept in the refrigerator where they will keep for 2 or 3 days.

MAKES ABOUT 1.4KG/3LB

900g/2lb strawberries
450g/1lb sugar with pectin
juice of 1 lemon

Place the strawberries in a non-metallic bowl and crush with a wooden spoon. Stir in the sugar, then cover and place in an oven preheated to its lowest setting until warm but not hot. Remove the bowl and leave to stand for for 1 hour, stirring occasionally, until the sugar has dissolved.

Stir in the lemon juice, then pack into small freezerproof containers, leaving plenty of headroom to allow for expansion during freezing. Cover and seal (see pages 12-13).

Leave to stand at a cool temperature for 6 hours, then refrigerate for 24-48 hours until jellied. Store in the freezer. Return to room temperature 1 hour before serving.

Warm and pour over baked or steamed sponge puddings; spoon over ice cream or eat with plain yogurt or fromage frais.

Variation: *Freezer Raspberry Jam*
Substitute raspberries for the strawberries.

Freezer jams: these are not boiled like ordinary jams, so they have a softer set. They have a particularly fresh and delicious flavour.

Strawberry and Rhubarb Jam

I first tasted strawberries and rhubarb together in a pie filling and have since combined them in a jam.

MAKES ABOUT 2KG/4½LB

450g/1lb strawberries, halved if large
1.4kg/3lb rhubarb, cut into 1.25cm/½in
** lengths**
1.4kg/3lb warmed sugar (see page 7)
3 lemons, halved

Layer the fruit and sugar in a non-metallic bowl. Squeeze the lemons, reserving the pips and skins. Pour the juice over the fruit and sugar, cover and leave in a cool place overnight.

Chop the lemon halves, then tie them in a muslin bag with the pips. Pour the fruit mixture into a pan and add the muslin bag. If the sugar has not dissolved, heat gently until it does. Bring quickly to the boil and boil rapidly for about 15 minutes, stirring as necessary, until setting point is reached (see page 17).

Remove the pan from the heat and skim the scum from the surface with a slotted spoon. Discard the bag. Leave the jam to stand for 10-15 minutes. Stir gently and ladle into warm, clean, dry jars. Cover and seal (see pages 12-13). Leave overnight to set. Store in a cool, dark, dry place.

Blackcurrant Jam

With its rich, full, fruity flavour and its strong, dark colour, this blackcurrant jam is one of my favourite jams.

MAKES ABOUT 2.5KG/5¼LB

1.4kg/3lb blackcurrants
2kg/4½lb warmed sugar (see page 7)

ℬLACKCURRANTS

Put the blackcurrants in a pan with 1.1 litres/2 pints water and bring to the boil. Lower the heat and simmer, stirring occasionally, for 45-60 minutes until the fruit skins are soft and the water reduced by about one-third.

Over a low heat stir in the sugar until it has completely dissolved, then raise the heat and boil hard for 6-8 minutes, stirring occasionally until setting point is reached (see page 17).

Remove from the heat and skim the scum from the surface of with a slotted spoon. Ladle into warm, clean, dry jars. Cover and seal (see pages 12-13). Leave overnight to set. Store in a cool, dark, dry place.

Blackcurrant Cordial

When you make your own blackcurrant cordial there is no need to worry about it containing additives or preservatives.

MAKES ABOUT 900ML/1½ PINTS

1.8kg/4lb blackcurrants
350-425g/12-15oz sugar
1½ lemons

Gently heat the blackcurrants and 300ml/ 10fl oz water in a large pan for about 20 minutes, crushing the blackcurrants occasionally with a wooden spoon.

Press the contents of the pan through a non-metallic sieve. Measure the juice and pour it back into the rinsed pan. Add 225-300g/8-10oz sugar and the juice of 1 lemon for every 570ml/1 pint juice and heat gently, stirring, until the sugar has dissolved. Raise the heat and boil for 1 minute.

Skim the scum from the surface with a slotted spoon, then pour the cordial into warm, clean, dry bottles, leaving a 1.25cm/ ½in headspace. Cover, then loosen the lid by half a turn. Process in a boiling waterbath (see page 13) for 25 minutes. Remove the bottles from the water bath and tighten the lids immediately. Store in a cool, dark, dry place for up to 6 months.

As well as using as the base for drinks (try adding 1 or 2 crushed mint leaves to drinks), blackcurrant cordial can be poured over pears, ice cream, fresh unsalted soft cheese, and stirred into crème fraîche or Greek yogurt. A decoration of mint looks particularly enticing.

Left: Blackcurrant Cordial makes a deliciously refreshing summertime drink.

Spiced Redcurrant Jelly with Drambuie

This is an ideal way of rescuing flavourless commercial redcurrant jelly. The spices continue to flavour the jelly after potting, so if you keep the jelly for long you may want to remove the cinnamon and perhaps the cloves after a while (gently warming the jelly is the best way to do this). Pink peppercorns are not related to black peppercorns and have more of an aromatic, pine flavour than a peppery one.

MAKES ABOUT 350G/12OZ

thinly pared zest of 1 lemon, cut into fine shreds
350g/12oz jar redcurrant jelly
juice of 1 lemon
3 tablespoons Drambuie
seeds from 2 cardamom pods, crushed
4 cloves
1 cinnamon stick
¼-½ teaspoon pink peppercorns
freshly ground black pepper

Add the lemon shreds to a small saucepan of boiling water and boil for 10 minutes. Drain and refresh under running cold water. Drain and dry on paper towels.

Gently melt the redcurrant jelly with the lemon juice and shreds and 2 tablespoons Drambuie, stirring until smooth. Add the spices and pepper and boil hard for 4 minutes until setting point is reached (see page 17).

Remove from the heat, add the remaining Drambuie and leave to stand for 10-15 minutes. Ladle the jelly into a warm, clean, dry jar. Cover and seal (see pages 12-13). Leave overnight to set. Store in a cool, dark, dry place.

Serve with cold ham, cold game pies, or venison; eat French-style with plain soft cheeses or plain crisp biscuits for dessert.

Superlative Redcurrant Jelly

This easy no-cook recipe is my favourite way of making redcurrant jelly, as it preserves the clear, fresh taste of the fruit. It has a lighter set than other redcurrant jellies; just how runny it is will depend on the amount of pectin and acid in the currants. (If you would like a firmer set, boil the juice and dissolved sugar until setting point is reached.) Unfortunately this jelly does not keep as long as some jellies, so it's one of the preserves I use first rather than one I hang on to for months. If you don't have somewhere nice and cool to keep it, the warmest part of the refrigerator, such as the salad drawer, is probably the best place.

1.4-1.6kg/3-3½lb redcurrants
500g/18oz warmed sugar (see page 7)
 (see page 7)

Purée the redcurrants by pressing them through a non-metallic sieve or blending them and then pouring them through the sieve, then tip into a scalded jelly bag set over a large non-metallic bowl and leave to strain, undisturbed, in a cool place for 8-12 hours.

Preheat the oven to a low to moderate heat – the exact temperature is not important. Measure the strained juice into a heatproof bowl, and add 350g/12oz sugar for every 570ml/1 pint juice. Put the bowl in the oven until the mixture is really hot. Pour the redcurrant juice into a warm, deep saucepan and vigorously stir with a wooden spoon until the sugar has dissolved and the mixture has slightly stiffened.

Remove the pan from the heat and remove any scum from the surface with a slotted spoon. Immediately ladle the jelly into warm, clean, dry jars. Cover and seal (see pages 12-13). Leave overnight to set. Store in a cool, dark, dry place.

Redcurrant Gin

MAKES ABOUT 1.9 LITRES/2¾ PINTS

600g/1¼lb redcurrants
300g/10oz caster sugar
750ml/27fl oz bottle of gin

Crush the redcurrants with the sugar, then transfer the mixture to a jar. Pour in the gin, cover, seal and shake the jar. Leave in a cool, dark, dry place for 3 months, shaking the jar every day for 4 weeks, then only occasionally.

Strain the gin, if liked, and pour into clean bottles. Alternatively, serve the gin by pouring it off through a muslin-lined non-metallic sieve, and top up the jar with more fruit and sugar as the level goes down. Sieve to serve.

Variations: *Raspberry Gin*
Follow the recipe but there is no need to crush the berries. Simply put all the ingredients in a jar. If available, use vanilla-flavoured sugar. Makes about 1.9 litres/2¾ pints.
Blackberry Gin
Use ripe fruit and follow the recipe, simply substituting blackberries for redcurrants. There is no need to crush the berries. Makes about 1.9 litres/2¾ pints.

Serve after meals or as an evening warmer.

Summer Fruits in Kirsch

In France this is known as *confiture de vieux garçons* (bachelors' jam). This is, I suppose, because it is extremely easy to make, requires no cooking and is alcoholic. I'm sure plenty of bachelors will be affronted at these implications; I'm equally sure that there are many non-bachelors to whom this recipe will appeal.

𝒮UMMER FRUITS

Other fruits, such as cherries, apricots, peaches and nectarines, can also be used, but make sure you prick them first if using them whole. You won't, however, get many of the last two in each jar – instead halve, quarter or thickly slice them, peeling them too, if liked.

MAKES ABOUT 450G/1LB

450g/1lb prepared summer fruits, such as strawberries, raspberries, loganberries and red- and blackcurrants
175g/6oz caster sugar
300-400ml/10-14fl oz kirsch

Layer the fruit and sugar in a clean, dry preserving jar or other wide-necked jar and leave for 2 hours.

Pour enough kirsch into the jar to cover the fruit. Cover and seal the jar (see pages 12-13). Store in a cool, dark, dry place for at least 1 month before eating, turning the jar upside down every week or so.

Red Summer Fruits Preserve

Capture the taste and memories of summer with this delicious and attractive preserve. I like to use raspberry *eau-de-vie* to intensify and fortify the flavour. Raspberry, strawberry or cherry brandy will also add colour and sweetness.

MAKES ABOUT 1.6KG/3½LB

675g/1½lb raspberries
6 tablespoons lemon juice
150ml/5fl oz freshly squeezed orange juice
1.4kg/3lb warmed sugar (see page 7)
900g/2lb mixed red summer fruits, such as loganberries, redcurrants, strawberries and stoned red cherries
4 tablespoons raspberry *eau-de-vie* (see above)

In a pan, gently cook the raspberries in the lemon and orange juices for 5-10 minutes until soft. Push through a non-metallic sieve and return to the rinsed pan.

Stir in the warmed sugar over a low heat until dissolved then add the remaining fruit, raise the heat and boil hard for 10-15 minutes, stirring as necessary, until setting point is reached.

Above: Red Summer Fruits Preserve makes an appropriately light filling for a light sponge cake.

Remove from the heat, skim any scum from the surface and stir in the *eau-de-vie*. Leave for 10 minutes, then stir and ladle into warm, clean, dry jars. Cover and seal (see pages 12-13). Leave overnight to set. Store in a cool, dark, dry place.

Roast Loin of Pork with Gooseberry Sauce

SERVES 4

2 tablespoons fresh white breadcrumbs
about 8 tablespoons Gooseberry Sauce
 (see below)
1.4kg/3lb loin of pork, boned
olive oil, for rubbing joint
175-225ml/6-8fl oz medium-bodied dry
 white wine
salt and freshly ground black pepper

Heat the oven to 180°C/350°F/gas mark 4.

In a small bowl, combine the breadcrumbs with 2 tablespoons gooseberry sauce.

Weigh the pork loin, then season the inside. Spread thinly with the gooseberry sauce mixture. Roll up the loin and tie into shape. Score the rind deeply and rub with oil and salt to produce good crackling.

Place the joint in a roasting tin and roast for 30 minutes per 450g/1lb, plus 30 minutes extra.

Transfer the pork to a warm plate and keep warm. Spoon the fat from the roasting tin, then stir the wine into the sediment. Boil until most of the wine has evaporated, then stir in the remaining gooseberry sauce. Season and serve with the pork.

Gooseberry Sauce

Although customarily made with a brown sugar, this sauce can be made with white, in which case it can be served with grilled mackerel, or deep-fried Camembert.

MAKES ABOUT 1.1 LITRES/2 PINTS

900g/2lb green gooseberries
450ml/16fl oz Spiced Vinegar (see page 139)
675g/1½lb warmed demerara or soft light
 brown sugar (see page 7)
1 teaspoon ground cinnamon

Put the fruit and vinegar in a saucepan and bring to the boil, then simmer for 10-15 minutes until tender. Purée in a blender or press through a fine non-metallic sieve, and return the purée to the rinsed pan.

Add the warmed sugar and the cinnamon to the puréed gooseberries, and heat, stirring, until the sugar has dissolved. Raise

Above: Roast Loin of Pork is both stuffed and served with Gooseberry Sauce.

the heat and simmer for 10-15 minutes, stirring frequently, to make a thick sauce.

Pour the sauce into warm, clean, dry jars. Cover and seal (see pages 12-13). Store in a cool, dark, dry place.

Gooseberries, Figs

Gooseberry and Raspberry Jam

Raspberry and gooseberry jams are notorious for their pips, so here is a smooth, pip- and skin-free jam. (This does mean that the yield is less than if the fruit were left unsieved which you can, of course, do.) It is also a very fruity jam as the fruit is heated without any water until tender in a low oven, and sugar with pectin is used to minimize the boiling-to-set time (you will need to stir the jam frequently during this time).

MAKES ABOUT 1.8KG/3¾LB

900g/2lb ripe gooseberries
675g/1½lb raspberries
about 1.4kg/3lb warmed sugar with pectin
 (see page 7)

Put the fruit in a heavy oven-proof dish, cover and place in the oven set to its lowest temperature (the bottom oven of an Aga is ideal), mashing the fruit occasionally with a wooden spoon, until soft.

 Press the fruit through a non-metallic sieve with a wooden spoon, pressing down well on the skins, pips and pulp to push through as much extract as possible.

 Weigh the extract and put into a pan with an equal weight of sugar with pectin. Heat gently, stirring, until the sugar has dissolved. Raise the heat and boil hard for at least 4 minutes, stirring frequently, until setting point is reached (see page 17).

 Remove the pan from the heat and skim any scum from the surface with a slotted spoon. Leave the jam to stand for 10-15 minutes, then ladle it into warm, clean, dry jars. Cover and seal (see pages 12-13). Leave overnight to set. Store in a cool, dark, dry place.

Fig Conserve

This has a good fresh, fruity taste as it is not cooked for long, which preserves the delicate, scented flavour. The low sugar content makes it quite runny and means it does not keep long, so use it within 3 months. Choose fruit that is not too ripe.

MAKES ABOUT 1.6KG/3½LB

2 lemons
2 cloves
900g/2lb figs, quartered
450g/1lb warmed sugar (see page 7)

Grate the zest from the lemons and squeeze out the juice, reserving the pips. Tie the pips and the cloves in a square of muslin using a long piece of string. Tie the other end of the string to the handle of a pan so the bag is suspended just above the bottom of the pan. Add the lemon juice, figs and 150ml/5fl oz water to the pan and simmer for about 15 minutes until the figs are tender. Remove the muslin bag.

 Over a low heat, stir in the warmed sugar and the lemon zest until the sugar has dissolved. Raise the heat and boil hard, stirring occasionally, for about 40 minutes until thick and syrupy.

Preparing figs: quarter figs lengthways to display the attractive, deep red interiors to their best advantage.

Remove from the heat and skim the scum from the surface with a slotted spoon. Leave the conserve to stand for 10-15 minutes. Stir gently, then ladle into warm, clean, dry jars. Cover and seal (see pages 12-13). Leave overnight to set. Store in a cool, dark, dry place, and refrigerate after opening.

Spiced Figs

Don't waste succulent ripe figs on this recipe but use those that are not good enough to eat raw. As compensation, you will have a sweet-sour-spicy treat in store.

MAKES ABOUT 1KG/2¼LB

250g/9oz caster sugar
2 tablespoons clear honey
425ml/15fl oz white wine vinegar
3 cloves
6 black peppercorns
2 cinnamon sticks
1.25cm/½in piece of fresh ginger, thinly sliced
3 allspice berries
pared zest of 1 lemon
675g/1½lb ripe but firm figs, thickly sliced

Gently heat the sugar, honey and vinegar together in a pan, stirring, until the sugar has dissolved. Add the spices and lemon zest and boil for 1½ minutes. Remove the pan from the heat and add the figs. Return to the heat and bring to the boil, then simmer for 1 minute, pushing the fruit under the vinegar.

 Carefully pour the figs, spices and vinegar into a non-metallic bowl, cover and leave to stand overnight.

 Using a slotted spoon, pack the fig slices tightly into a clean, dry jar.

 Boil the spiced vinegar for 15 minutes until reduced to 150ml/5fl oz. Pour into the jar, cover immediately with a vinegar-proof lid and seal (see pages 12-13). Store in a cool, dark, dry place for 1 week before using.

$\mathscr{S}$TONE $\mathscr{F}$RUITS

*Stone fruits come from places as diverse as the orchards
of the English countryside, the humid regions of
southern India and the warm terraces
of the Mediterranean coast. Their
enormous variety ranges from
exotic, luscious mangoes to
inedible-when-raw sloes.
In Britain, cherries start the
stone fruit year in June, followed by peaches and
nectarines from the Mediterranean as the summer
progresses. Then come damsons and plums, but it is
not until a while later, in October, that sloes are ready
for picking. Fresh dates, mainly from Israel, are picked
in the autumn, but can be stored so that they are
available year round. Mangoes, too, are always in
season somewhere in the world, as different varieties
come into season at different times. Although guavas
have seeds not stones, I have included a recipe for
Guava Jelly (see page 109) in this chapter as it
seemed the most appropriate place.*

*Left (from left to right): Plum Jelly, Spiced Plums, Apricot and
Amaretto Conserve and Nectarines in White Wine Syrup.*

Chunky Apricot Chutney

This chunky chutney (the apricots are not cooked down) is fruity, mild and refined.

MAKES ABOUT 1.2-1.4KG/2½-3LB

1kg/2¼lb ripe apricots, halved and stoned
115g/4oz raisins
1 onion, finely chopped
2-3 garlic cloves, quite finely chopped
1 teaspoon coriander seeds, crushed
1¼ teaspoons grated fresh ginger
2 tablespoons sea salt
300g/10oz soft light brown sugar
300ml/10fl oz white wine vinegar

Put all the ingredients in a saucepan and heat gently, stirring, until the sugar has dissolved. Raise the heat and boil, stirring occasionally, until the apricots are completely soft but not disintegrating.

Using a slotted spoon, transfer the apricots to warm, clean, dry jars and keep warm in a low oven.

Boil the liquid remaining in the pan hard until it becomes a thick syrup. Ladle into the jars, cover and seal with vinegar-proof lids (see pages 12-13). Store in a cool, dark, dry place for 1 month before eating.

Apricots in Cointreau

MAKES ABOUT 1.5 LITRES/2½ PINTS

675g/1½lb ripe, large, well-flavoured apricots
350g/12oz caster sugar
300ml/10fl oz Cointreau
about 250ml/9fl oz brandy or whisky

Prick the apricots all over with a darning needle or wooden cocktail stick, then layer them with the sugar in a clean, dry jar.

Mix together the Cointreau and brandy and pour into the jar to cover the fruit. Swivel the jar to dislodge any air bubbles, then seal and shake the jar (see pages 12-13).

Store in a cool, dark, dry place for at least 2 months before eating; shake the jar occasionally during the first week or so until the sugar has completely dissolved.

Fresh Apricot Jam

You need to use top-quality apricots for jam-making, and finding fruit of this calibre is not always easy. Any fruits that are woolly and lacking in flavour will make a poor-quality jam. Fruit that is not ripe enough to eat can, of course, be used. A warm, glowing sheen indicates a good flavour.

MAKES ABOUT 1.4KG/3LB

900g/2lb well-flavoured apricots
juice of 1 small lemon
1 teaspoon grated lemon zest
900g/2lb warmed sugar (see page 7)

Halve the apricots, reserving several of the stones. Crack the reserved stones with nutcrackers, a rolling pin or a hammer. Remove the kernels and blanch them in boiling water for 1-2 minutes. Drain the kernels and slip off the skins.

Put the kernels into a pan with the

Preparing apricot kernels: blanch the kernels in boiling water and drain. The skins should now slip off quite easily.

apricots, lemon juice and zest and 200ml/7fl oz water. Bring to the boil, then simmer until tender.

Over a low heat, stir in the warmed sugar until it has dissolved. Raise the heat and boil hard, stirring occasionally, until setting point is reached (see page 17).

Remove the pan from the heat and skim any scum from the surface with a slotted spoon. Leave the jam to stand for 10-15 minutes. Stir gently, then ladle the jam into warm, clean, dry jars. Cover and seal (see pages 12-13). Leave overnight to set. Store in a cool, dark, dry place.

Apricot and Amaretto Conserve

MAKES ABOUT 900G/2LB

675g/1½lb fresh apricots
675g/1½lb vanilla sugar
3 tablespoons Amaretto liqueur

Halve the apricots and remove the stones. Crack the stones with a rolling pin or a hammer. Remove the kernels and blanch them in boiling water for 1-2 minutes. Drain and slip off the skins.

Layer the apricots and sugar in a non-metallic bowl, cover and leave overnight in a cool place, by which time most of the sugar should have dissolved.

Tip the contents of the bowl into a pan, add 150ml/5fl oz water and the kernels and heat gently, stirring, until any remaining sugar has dissolved. Raise the heat and boil hard for 15-20 minutes, stirring occasionally, until slightly thickened.

Remove from the heat. Skim any scum off the surface, then stir in the Amaretto and leave for 10-15 minutes. Stir and ladle into warm, clean, dry jars. Cover and seal (see pages 12-13). Leave overnight to set. Store in a cool, dark, dry place.

Light and Lovely Apricot Pudding

This steamed pudding can provide a treat at a dinner party as well as a family lunch.

SERVES 4

Apricot and Amaretto Conserve (see page 96)
1½ tablespoons lemon juice
75g/3oz butter, diced
100g/3½oz fresh white breadcrumbs
generous ¼ teaspoon bicarbonate of soda
20g/¾oz self-raising flour
50g/2oz demerara sugar
40g/1½oz plain chocolate, finely chopped
 (optional)
2 eggs, size 3, lightly beaten

Line the bottom of a buttered 570-700ml/ 1-1¼ pint pudding basin using apricot halves from the conserve, placed cut sides up.

In a pan gently heat 4 tablespoons of the jelly from the conserve with the lemon juice and butter until the butter has melted.

Meanwhile, mix together the dry ingredients in a bowl. Stir in the butter mixture then slowly pour in the eggs, mixing thoroughly. Spoon into the basin, taking care not to dislodge the apricots.

Make a pleat across the centre of a piece of buttered foil and put it loosely over the basin to allow the pudding to rise. Tie the foil in place with string round the basin rim and use the string to form a loose handle across the top of the foil. Put the basin in a steaming basket. Cover and place over a saucepan of boiling water and steam for about 1¾ hours, until just set in the centre.

Lift out of the basket. Remove the string and foil. Run a knife round the basin sides to loosen the pudding, place a plate over the bowl, then turn the bowl upside down.

Left: golden Apricot and Amaretto Conserve is used to top this sumptuous Light and Lovely Apricot Pudding.

Apricot Brandy

MAKES ABOUT 850ML/1½ PINTS

12 large ripe, well-flavoured apricots
225g/8oz caster sugar
570ml/1 pint brandy

Halve the apricots, reserving the stones. Cut the flesh into small pieces and put into a jar. Crack the stones with nutcrackers, a rolling pin or a hammer. Remove the kernels, blanch them in boiling water for 1-2 minutes, then drain and slip off the skins (see page 96).

Add the kernels to the jar with the sugar. Pour in the brandy, then seal the jar and shake to dissolve the sugar.

Store in a cool, dark, dry place for 2 months before using, shaking the jar every couple of days. Strain off the brandy and pour into clean, dry bottles. Cover and seal (see pages 12-13). Eat the fruit separately.

Variation: *Cherry Brandy*
Trim the stalks, if necessary, from 450g/1lb cherries to 0.5cm/¼in of the fruit. Prick the cherries well with a darning needle and layer in a wide-necked jar with 75g/3oz sugar. Pour in the brandy and proceed as above. Makes about 800ml/1½ pints.

Apricot Cordial

Use a fairly good-quality brandy for this recipe as a cheap one would spoil the cordial; white rum, gin or vodka can be substituted. The strained apricots can be eaten as they are, used to fill crêpes or made into a mousse or soufflé.

MAKES ABOUT 1.6 LITRES/2¾ PINTS

250g/9oz well-flavoured dried apricots,
 coarsely chopped
500ml/18fl oz dry white wine
150g/5oz clear honey
150ml/5fl oz brandy

Leave the apricots to macerate in the wine in a covered non-metallic bowl for about 12 hours.

Tip the contents of the bowl into a saucepan and bring slowly to the simmering point. Stir in the honey until it has dissolved, then remove the pan from the heat, cover and leave to cool.

Pour the contents of the pan into the bowl in which the apricots were macerated, cover and leave in a cool place, but not the refrigerator, for 3 days, stirring occasionally.

Strain off the liquid and stir in the brandy. Pour into clean, dry bottles. Cover and seal (see pages 12-13). Store in a cool, dark, dry place for 2 months before drinking.

As well as being a drink, a few spoonfuls of this cordial are wonderful in any fresh or dried fruit salad, over ice cream, with crêpes or waffles and with freshly baked tarte tatin.

Nectarine Conserve

An elegant, delicately-flavoured conserve to make in the height of summer when nectarines are at their most succulent, sun-ripened best. Add a couple of spoonfuls or so of an orange liqueur or brandy, if liked, after removing the cooked conserve from the heat.

MAKES ABOUT 1.4KG/3LB

1.1kg/2½lb ripe but firm nectarines
675g/1½lb warmed sugar (see page 7)
2 tablespoons lime juice

Peel the nectarines, reserving the skins. Halve and stone the fruit and layer the fruit with the sugar in a non-metallic bowl, cover and leave overnight, by which time most of the sugar will have dissolved.

Put the nectarine skins in a saucepan, just cover with water and boil until the water is reduced to a thin layer at the bottom of the pan. Press the contents of the pan through a non-metallic sieve into another pan.

Pour the contents of the bowl into the pan, add the lime juice and heat gently, stirring, until any remaining sugar has dissolved. Raise the heat and boil hard for 15-20 minutes or until slightly thickened.

Remove from the heat and leave to stand for 10-15 minutes until the nectarines remain suspended in the syrup when stirred. Ladle into warm, clean, dry jars taking care not to trap any air bubbles. Cover and seal (see pages 12-13). Leave overnight to set. Store in a cool, dark, dry place.

Nectarine Butter

Simmering nectarines into a fruit butter really concentrates their flavour to make a memorable teatime or breakfast spread. Make this when nectarines are plentiful.

MAKES ABOUT 450G/1LB

900g/2lb ripe nectarines, peeled, stoned
 and chopped
warmed sugar (see page 7)

Gently simmer the nectarines in 450ml/ 16fl oz water, stirring occasionally, until soft. Press through a non-metallic sieve with a wooden spoon.

Weigh the purée and return to the rinsed pan. Stir in 115g/4oz sugar for every 225g/ 8oz purée and stir over a low heat until the sugar has dissolved. Raise the heat and boil for 30-45 minutes, stirring occasionally to start with, but then more frequently until the stirring is constant and the mixture resembles thick double cream.

Spoon into warm, clean, dry jars; do not trap any air bubbles. Cover and seal (see pages 12-13). Store in a cool, dark, dry place for a few days before eating.

NECTARINES

Freezer Nectarine Jam

This is a quick and easy way to preserve the best of the summer nectarines.

MAKES ABOUT 1.3KG/2¾LB

**900g/2lb ripe nectarines, peeled, stoned
 and coarsely chopped
900g/2lb sugar with pectin
juice of 1 lemon**

Thoroughly mix the nectarines, sugar and lemon juice together in a non-metallic bowl, place in an oven set to its lowest temperature to warm through gently. Remove from the oven, cover and leave for 8 hours, stirring occasionally until you are sure all the sugar has dissolved.

Ladle into freezerproof plastic containers, leaving a good headspace to allow for expansion during freezing, then cover and put in the refrigerator for 24-48 hours until the jam sets. Freeze for up to 6 months.

Bring the jam to room temperature 1 hour before serving. This jam will keep in the refrigerator for up to 2 days after opening.

Nectarines in White Wine Syrup

While this recipe does not demand a really good wine, do not use a thin acidic one. You can add a small bunch of scented geranium leaves or lemon balm, or some scented rose petals in place of the orange peel.

MAKES 1.8G/4LB

**350g/12oz sugar
2 strips of orange peel
700ml/1¼ pints dry white wine
12 ripe but firm nectarines, peeled and halved
brandy**

In a pan, gently heat the sugar and orange peel in the wine, stirring until the sugar has dissolved. Bring to just on simmering point and simmer gently for 8 minutes.

Add the nectarine halves to the syrup, in batches if necessary, and poach for 10 minutes until tender.

Using a slotted spoon, pack the fruit into warm, clean, dry jars. Boil the syrup for 1 minute, remove the orange peel and pour the syrup over the fruit. Add brandy to cover the nectarines. Cover and seal (see pages 12-13). Store in a cool, dark, dry place for 1 month before using.

Serve lightly chilled and topped with fromage frais, Greek yogurt, cream or mascarpone cheese and sprinkled with toasted flaked almonds; to top a tart filled with crème pâtissière; with almond pancakes.

Left: Nectarines in White Wine Syrup are delicious served slightly chilled with mascarpone cheese and toasted flaked almonds.

Peach and Honeysuckle Cheese

I now have honeysuckle growing outside windows on two sides of my kitchen. One catches the morning sun, the other the afternoon and early evening sun so the strong, yet delicate scent pervades the room throughout the day. In this cheese, I have captured some of the magic to give real indulgence on a winter's day. This recipe needs less boiling time than some other cheeses.

MAKES ABOUT 600G/1¼LB

900g/2lb peaches
1 firmly packed cup honeysuckle flowers
juice of 1 lemon
warmed sugar (see page 7)

Halve, stone and slice the peaches without peeling them. Crack a few of the stones with nutcrackers, a rolling pin or a hammer and remove the kernels. Blanch the kernels in boiling water for 1-2 minutes, then slip off the skins (see page 96).

Put the peaches, kernels, honeysuckle and lemon juice in a pan. Add water to just cover and bring to the boil, then simmer gently, covered, for about 20 minutes until the peaches are very soft.

Tip the contents of the pan into a scalded jelly bag suspended over a non-metallic bowl and leave to strain, undisturbed, in a cool place for 8-12 hours.

Weigh the juice and add 350g/12oz sugar for every 570ml/1pint juice. Heat gently, stirring, until the sugar has dissolved then simmer gently for 40-45 minutes, stirring frequently, until the mixture is so thick and dry that the spoon leaves a clean line when drawn through it.

Spoon into clean, warm, dry jars or lightly oiled decorative moulds. Cover and seal (see pages 12-13). Store in a cool, dark, dry place for at least 2-3 months before eating.

Serve Peach and Honeysuckle Cheese with unsalted, full-fat soft cheese and crisp sweet biscuits to make an instant and unusual dessert; serve on fresh, crusty bread for a delicious breakfast.

Above: this Peach and Honeysuckle Cheese captures the heady scents of a summer's day.

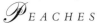

Peaches

Peach and Raspberry Jam

Peaches and raspberries make a beautiful duo, as immortalized by the great chef, Escoffier, when he created Pêches Melba in honour of the famous opera singer, Dame Nelly Melba.

MAKES ABOUT 2KG/4½LB

1.2kg/2lb 10oz peaches
2 tablespoons lemon juice
1kg/2¼lb raspberries
1.4kg/3lb warmed sugar (see page 7)

Peel the peaches and put the peel on a square of muslin. Halve the peaches and extract the stones. Crack the stones with nutcrackers, a rolling pin or a hammer and remove the kernels. Add the kernels to the peach peel and tie the muslin into a bag. Put 125ml/4½fl oz water and the lemon juice into a pan. Chop the peaches, then add to the pan and tie the loose end of the muslin bag string on to the pan handle so it is suspended in the mixture. Bring the mixture to the boil, lower the heat and simmer for about 20 minutes until the peaches are soft.

Remove the pan from the heat and, using a slotted spoon, lift out the muslin bag and press it hard with the back of a metal spoon, so that the juices run into the pan. Add the raspberries to the pan and return it to the heat, then simmer for 5 minutes.

Stir the warmed sugar into the pan over a low heat until dissolved, then raise the heat and boil hard for 10-15 minutes, until setting point is reached (see page 17).

Remove from the heat and skim the scum from the surface with a slotted spoon. Ladle into warm, clean, dry jars. Cover and seal (see pages 12-13). Leave overnight to set. Store in a cool, dark, dry place.

Use with cream to layer a sponge cake.

Peach Marmalade

I love this marmalade and never tire of eating it at any time of day. Adjust the cooking time of the orange if you like so that the peel is cooked as tender or as firm as you like.

MAKES ABOUT 1KG/2¼LB

2 large, thin-skinned oranges, very thinly sliced
1kg/2¼lb peaches, peeled, halved, stoned and chopped
juice of 1 lemon
675g/1½lb warmed sugar (see page 7)

Halve each orange slice, then cut each piece into quarters, reserving the pips. Tie the pips in a muslin bag. Put the orange pieces, the muslin bag and 200ml/7fl oz water in a smallish saucepan, cover and simmer gently for about 40 minutes until the peel is tender.

Tip the contents of the pan into a preserving pan and tie the loose end of the muslin bag string on to the pan handle so the bag is suspended in the mixture. Add the peaches and lemon juice and simmer, until tender. Lift out the muslin bag with a slotted spoon and press hard it with the back of a metal spoon so that the juices run back into the pan. Discard the bag.

Peeling peaches: pour boiling water over the peaches and leave for 10-30 seconds, depending on their ripeness, before peeling.

Over a low heat, stir in the warmed sugar until it has dissolved. Raise the heat and boil hard for 10-15 minutes until setting point is reached (see page 17). Ladle into warm, clean, dry jars. Cover and seal (see pages 12-13). Leave overnight to set. Store in a cool, dark, dry place.

Serve this lovely marmalade for a Continental breakfast of warmed croissants and brioches, or at teatime. It is also good with fresh cream as a filling for sponge cakes.

Spiced Peaches

This particular blend of spices gives the peaches a slightly exotic taste.

MAKES 1.1 LITRES/2 PINTS

900g/2lb sugar
570ml/1 pint white wine vinegar
2 cinnamon sticks
12 black peppercorns
4 cardamom pods, crushed
1 teaspoon cloves
2 star anise
1.8kg/4lb peaches, peeled, halved and stoned

In a pan, gently heat the sugar in the vinegar with the spices, stirring, until the sugar has dissolved. Raise the heat and boil for 2-2½ minutes. Add the peach halves and simmer for 4-5 minutes until they are tender.

Using a slotted spoon, transfer the peaches to a clean, warm, dry jar. Reduce the liquid slightly by boiling it for 2-3 minutes, then pour over the peaches. Swivel the jar to expel any air bubbles, then cover and seal (see pages 12-13). Store in a cool, dark, dry place for 2 months before eating.

Serve the peaches with turkey, duck, pork or cold ham.

Black Cherry Jam with Kirsch

The cherries for this jam must be acidic Morello cherries, not just any black variety. But even these are very low in pectin so I use sugar with pectin to encourage a good set and keep the cooking time down. You can use paler Duke cherries instead, if you prefer. Kirsch sets off the cherry flavour well.

MAKES ABOUT 1.4KG/3LB

900g/2lb black Morello cherries, stoned
1kg/2¼lb sugar with pectin
1 tablespoon kirsch

In a pan, gently heat the cherries, sugar and 1 tablespoon water until the sugar has dissolved, then simmer until the cherries are just tender.

Raise the heat and bring to the boil, then boil hard for about 4 minutes until setting point is reached (see page 17).

Remove the pan from the heat and skim any scum that has formed on the surface with a slotted spoon. Stir the kirsch into the jam, then ladle it into warm, clean, dry jars. Cover and seal (see pages 12-13). Leave the jam overnight to set. Store in a cool, dark, dry place.

Serve as a topping for a cheesecake; in Black Forest gâteau; with cream in a chocolate roulade. For savoury uses, serve with roast or grilled duck or roast turkey, either hot or cold.

Spiced Cherries

The inspiration for these cherries came from the Italian preserve, *Amarena Fabbri*, available only from a few specialist grocers.

MAKES ABOUT 1.2KG/2½LB

8g/¼oz piece of fresh ginger
450g/1lb granulated sugar
2.5cm/1in piece of cinnamon stick
3 cloves
300ml/10fl oz red wine vinegar
900g/2lb Morello cherries, stoned

Bruise the ginger with the flat of a large knife on a chopping board.

In a pan, gently heat the sugar and spices in the vinegar until the sugar has dissolved. Add the cherries and simmer gently until they are tender.

Using a slotted spoon, transfer the cherries to a non-metallic sieve placed over a bowl. Boil the vinegar until reduced to a thick syrup, adding the juices collected in the bowl. Scoop out the spices with a slotted spoon.

Return the cherries to the syrup and bring to the boil, then pour into warm, clean, dry jars. Cover with vinegar-proof lids and seal (see pages 12-13). Store in a cool, dark, dry place for at least 2 weeks before using.

Extremely good with roast game, especially venison and hare, or added to casseroles.

Left (clockwise from top): pale Duke, Morello and black cherries.

Savoury Cherry Cheese

On a recent visit to a nearby country market, I found a small stall selling a variety of assorted preserves. Everything was sparkling and all the products looked delicious, so I bought a selection. The preserves were so good, in fact, that I went back to the same stall and managed to get the recipe for this cheese.

MAKES ABOUT 1KG/2¼LB

900g/2lb sour cherries, such as Morello or
Duke, stoned
225g/8oz plump raisins
2 teaspoons mixed spice
300ml/10fl oz cider vinegar
225g/8oz light soft brown sugar, warmed
(see page 7)
150g/5oz clear honey

Put the cherries, raisins, mixed spice and vinegar into a pan and bring to the boil, then simmer until the cherries are tender. Press the mixture through a non-metallic sieve with a wooden spoon, making sure you push as much through the sieve as possible.

Return the mixture to the rinsed pan and, over a low heat, stir in the sugar and honey until the sugar has dissolved. Raise the heat and bring to the boil, then lower the heat again and boil, stirring as necessary, for about 45-55 minutes until the mixture is so thick the spoon leaves a clear line when drawn through it.

Spoon the cheese into small warm, clean, dry jars or lightly oiled decorative moulds. Cover and seal (see pages 12-13). Store in a cool, dark, dry place for 2-3 months before eating.

Serve this cheese with game, lamb, cold ham or bacon.

CHERRIES

Cherries in Almond Syrup

Morello cherries are a traditional acidic variety, whereas Dukes are a sweet-sour hybrid, so use the ones that will produce the flavour you most enjoy.

Adding the cracked cherry stones when cooking the cherries imparts an almond flavour, but if you like you can always boost it further by pouring some almond liqueur into the bottles.

MAKES 3.3 LITRES/6 PINTS

1.4kg/3lb Morello or Duke cherries (see above)
625g/1lb 6oz sugar

Remove the stones from the cherries, reserving a small handful of the stones. Tie them in a square of muslin and hit firmly with a rolling pin to crack them.

In a pan, gently heat the sugar in 1.7 litres/3 pints water, stirring until the sugar has dissolved. Add the muslin bag (tying the loose end of the string to the pan handle so the bag is suspended in the mixture), raise the heat and boil for 5 minutes.

Add the cherries and cook over a moderate heat for 5 minutes. Using a slotted spoon, transfer the cherries to warm, clean, dry jars.

Boil the syrup for a further 5 minutes until slightly reduced then discard the muslin bag. Pour the syrup over the cherries, making sure they are completely covered. Cover and seal the jars (see pages 12-13). Process in a boiling waterbath (see page 13) for 10 minutes. Remove the jars from the heat, tighten the lids, then leave to cool and test the seals. Store in a cool, dark, dry place for 2-3 days before eating.

The cherries can be used in almost any sweet recipe calling for cherries – in pie fillings, pancakes and sweet omelette fillings, stirred into plain cake mixtures, added to strudel fillings, spooned over ice cream or included in ice cream sundaes.

Variation: *Peaches in Almond Syrup*
Peel, halve and stone the peaches. Follow the recipe above. Makes 3.3 litres/6 pints.

Above: Cherries in Almond Syrup makes a quick and delectable filling for a light dessert of almond pancakes.

Damson Jam

Cinnamon and orange highlight the spicy flavour of damsons. There is no need to stone the fruit before cooking and there is no need to worry about hurrying unduly when removing the stones after the jam has been cooked. A 10-15 minute delay is needed anyway before potting it, otherwise the fruit skins will float to the surface of the jam in the jars.

MAKES ABOUT 1.8KG/4LB

grated zest and juice of 3 oranges
1.1kg/2½lb damsons
1½ teaspoons ground cinnamon
1.1kg/2½lb warmed sugar (see page 7)

Make the orange juice up to 300ml/10fl oz with water then put in a pan with the damsons, cinnamon and orange zest and cook gently in the liquid for about 40 minutes until the fruit is very tender and the liquid well reduced.

Over a low heat, stir in the warmed sugar until it has dissolved. Raise the heat and boil for about 10 minutes, stirring occasionally, until setting point is reached (see page 17).

Remove from the heat and take out the damson stones with a slotted spoon. Put the stones into a non-metallic sieve over the pan to drain for about 15 minutes. Skim the surface with a slotted spoon. Stir the jam then ladle it into warm, clean, dry jars. Cover and seal (see pages 12-13). Leave overnight to set. Store in a cool, dark, dry place.

Variations: *Plum Jam*
Use 1.4kg/3lb plums, 300ml/10fl oz water and 1.4kg/3lb sugar. Halve and stone the plums, reserving about 14 of the stones. Crack the reserved plum stones (see page 108), remove the kernels and add them to the pan with the water and plums (the kernels add a complementary almond flavour). Simmer for 20-30 minutes until the plum skins are soft. Proceed with the recipe

above. Makes about 1.8kg/4¼lb.

Instead of adding the kernels, you could add orange zest and juice as in the recipe for Damson Jam.
Greengage Jam
Use 1.4kg/3lb greengages, 300ml/10fl oz water and 1.4kg/3lb sugar. Cook the whole greengages in the water until very soft, then proceed with the recipe above. Makes about 2.2kg/5lb.

Damson Cheese

This is a dark and richly flavoured cheese.

MAKES ABOUT 1.4KG/3LB

1.4kg/3lb damsons
warmed sugar (see page 7)

Just cover the damsons with water and simmer for 15-20 minutes until the fruit is very soft and no surplus water is visible. Scoop out the stones as they rise to the surface using a slotted spoon.

Press the damsons through a non-metallic sieve and measure the purée. Return the purée to the pan with 350g/12oz sugar for every 570ml/1 pint purée. Heat gently, stirring, until the sugar has dissolved, then boil gently, stirring frequently, for 45-55 minutes until the mixture is so thick that when the wooden spoon is drawn across the bottom of the pan, a clean line is left.

Spoon the cheese into warm, clean, dry jars or lightly-oiled small dishes or moulds. Cover and seal (see pages 12-13). Store the cheese in a cool, dark, dry place for 2-3 months before eating.

Serve with mature Cheddar cheese, or as an accompaniment to roast lamb, duck and game; with good, firm white bread and unsalted butter; moist parkin or dark ginger cake or with fresh soft cheese.

Sloe Gin

Blackthorn trees (the trees that bear sloes) grow in woods and along hedgerows. The small, dark, round fruits are traditionally not picked until after the first frost. It is advisable to wear gloves for this as the branches sport long spines. Sloes are too bitter for eating but they make a delicious warming, rich, red sloe gin that is not ready for drinking until the end of the year, and it is one of the traditional delights of Christmas. Just how much sugar you use is a matter of taste.

MAKES ABOUT 850ML/1½ PINTS

450g/1lb sloes, stalks discarded
75-115g/3-4oz sugar
a few blanched almonds, lightly crushed
1 bottle of gin

Prick each sloe all over with a darning needle, then layer with the sugar and almonds in a clean jar. Pour over the gin to cover the sloes completely.

Close the jar tightly, shake it well and leave in a cool dark, dry place for at least 3 months, shaking the jar occasionally.

Strain the gin through a non-metallic funnel lined with muslin, into clean, dry bottles. Seal the bottles (see pages 12-13). Store in a cool, dark, dry place.

As well as a warming drink, sloe gin can be used to liven up meat and game casseroles and sauces (see page 105).

Variations: *Sloe Vodka*
Use vodka in place of gin. Sloe vodka has a cleaner, fruitier taste than sloe gin. Makes about 850ml/1½ pints.
Damson Brandy
Use about 450g/1lb damsons and brandy instead of the sloes and gin and omit the almonds. Follow the main recipe. Makes about 850ml/1½ pints.

Pork with Sloe Gin Sauce

Sloe gin performs several roles in this special recipe – it gives a warm, slightly spicy flavour to the sauce, cuts through the creamy sauce and lifts the flavour of the sliced pork.

SERVES 6

900g/2lb pork tenderloin, cut into 1.25cm/ ½in thick slices
25g/1oz unsalted butter
2 tablespoons olive oil
1 shallot, chopped
125g/4½oz button mushrooms, sliced
300ml/10fl oz Sloe Gin (see page 104)
300ml/10fl oz beef stock
75g/3oz plump raisins
150ml/5fl oz crème fraîche or double cream
table salt and freshly ground black pepper

Heat the butter and oil in a heavy-based pan and brown the pork on both sides in batches. Remove with a slotted spoon and drain on paper towels.

Add the shallot and mushrooms to the pan and cook gently until softened but not coloured. Stir in the sloe gin to dislodge the sediment, then bring to the boil. Add the stock and raisins and return to simmering point, then add the pork, cover tightly and cook gently for 10-15 minutes until tender.

Transfer the pork to a warm serving dish, cover and keep warm. Boil the sauce hard until slightly reduced, then stir in the crème fraîche or cream and boil hard again until lightly syrupy. Season and pour over the pork while still hot.

Left: Sloe Gin combined with gently cooked shallots and raisins makes a richly flavoured sauce for this memorable pork dish.

Plum and Red Onion Confit

Szechuan peppercorns give a wonderful spicy-woody flavour to this confit. I give the onions just a short cooking on their own so they retain some texture at the end of the final cooking.

MAKES ABOUT 800G/1¾LB

450g/1lb red onions, chopped
2 tablespoons olive oil
1 tablespoon Szechuan peppercorns
675g/1½lb red plums, halved and stoned
300ml/10fl oz red wine vinegar
sea salt
115-175g/4-6oz soft brown sugar, warmed
 (see page 7)

Gently cook the onions in the oil in a heavy pan until they are as soft as you like.

Meanwhile, heat the peppercorns in a dry heavy-based frying pan until fragrant, moving them gently around the pan to prevent them from catching. Remove from the heat then tip the peppercorns into a mortar and crush finely with a pestle, or grind in a spice grinder or small blender.

Add the plums, peppercorns, vinegar and salt to the onions and simmer, uncovered, until the plums are tender.

Over a low heat, stir in the sugar until dissolved, then simmer until thick.

Spoon the confit into warm, clean, dry jars. Cover and seal (see pages 12-13). Store in a cool, dark, dry place for at least 1 month before eating.

With grilled or fried good-quality sausages and mashed potatoes; if the onions still have some bite left after the cooking, the relish can accompany mackerel.

Right: Plum and Red Onion Confit adds colour and spice to a dish of sausages and mash.

LUMS

Plum Jelly

MAKES 1.6-1.7KG/2¾-3LB

**1.4kg/3lb plums, halved and stoned
(see page 108)
1.4kg/3lb warmed sugar with pectin
(see page 7)**

Put the plums together with 850ml/1½ pints water into a pan and bring to the boil, then simmer gently for 20-30 minutes until the plums are tender.

Tip the contents of the pan into a scalded jelly bag suspended over a large non-metallic bowl and leave to strain, undisturbed, in a cool place for 8-12 hours.

Measure the strained juice – there should be about 1.2 litres/2½ pints. If there is not enough, make up the quantity with water; if there is too much, add an extra 85g/3oz sugar per 100ml/3½oz juice. Pour into the rinsed pan, add the sugar and heat gently, stirring, until the sugar has dissolved. Raise the heat and boil hard for 1 minute until the setting point is reached (see page 17).

Remove from the heat and skim any scum from the surface. Immediately ladle into warm clean, dry jars. Cover and seal (see pages 12-13). Leave overnight to set. Store in a cool, dark, dry place.

Plum Sauce

MAKES ABOUT 700ML/1¼ PINTS

**½ cinnamon stick
4 cloves
2 star anise
5 coriander seeds, lightly crushed
150ml/5fl oz cider vinegar
450g/1lb red or purple plums, stoned and
chopped (see page 108)
1 shallot, chopped
5 tablespoons each port and Madeira
juice each of ½ large lemon, ½ orange and
½ lime**

**pinch of five-spice powder
1 tablespoon redcurrant jelly
50g/2oz warmed demerara sugar (see page 7)**

Tie the cinnamon, cloves, star anise and coriander seeds in a muslin bag. Put the remaining ingredients except the sugar into a pan. Tie the loose string of the muslin bag on to the pan handle so the bag is suspended in the mixture. Bring to the boil, then simmer gently for about 45 minutes, stirring occasionally. Stir in the warmed sugar until it has dissolved, then continue to simmer gently for a further 45 minutes.

Discard the muslin bag, pour the sauce into a blender and mix to a purée. Pour the sauce into warm, clean, dry bottles. Cover and seal (see pages 12-13). Store in a cool, dark, dry place for 1 month before using.

Spiced Plums

The sweet spiced vinegar used here also works well with damsons, or, indeed, any other stone fruit.

MAKES ABOUT 2KG/4½LB

**1.3kg/2lb 14oz purple plums
675g/1½lb sugar**

**15g/½oz fresh ginger, grated
½ teaspoon cloves
½ teaspoon ground coriander seeds
½ teaspoon ground allspice
¼ cinnamon stick
450ml/16fl oz red wine vinegar**

Prick the fruit all over with a darning needle and put in a large pan so the fruit is no more than 2 layers deep.

In another pan, gently heat the sugar and spices in the vinegar, stirring until the sugar has dissolved. Raise the heat and bring to the boil, then simmer for 5 minutes.

Pour the spiced vinegar into the fruit pan and heat until boiling. Remove from the heat, cover and leave for about 8 hours.

Strain off the liquid through a non-metallic sieve and reserve. Using a slotted spoon, pack the fruit into warm, clean, dry jars. Boil the liquid hard until reduced by one-third then pour it into the jars to cover the fruit. Swivel the jars to dispel any air bubbles, then immediately cover the jars with vinegar-proof lids and seal (see pages 12-13). Store the plums in a cool, dark, dry place for 1 month before using.

Below (clockwise from top right): Victoria plums, red plums, greengages, damsons and Mirabelles.

Autumn Chutney

This chutney brings together the fruits of the orchard – apples, pears and plums. In the past, this type of chutney was made from the autumn harvest of fruits and put by in the pantry for serving with cold meats and cheeses in later months.

MAKES ABOUT 2KG/4½LB

450g/1lb Victoria plums, stoned (see below) and quite finely chopped
450g/1lb each pears and cooking apples, cored and cut into chunks without peeling
225g/8oz raisins
225g/8oz onions, quite finely chopped
finely grated peel and juice of 1 orange
570ml/1 pint cider vinegar
350g/12oz warmed light soft brown sugar (see page 7)
¼ teaspoon each ground cinnamon, ground ginger and ground cloves

Put the fruit, onions, orange zest and juice and the vinegar in a pan and bring to the boil, then simmer for about 45 minutes stirring occasionally, until the fruit is tender.

Over a low heat, stir in the warmed sugar and the spices until the sugar has dissolved. Then simmer, stirring occasionally, until the

Removing stones from plums: cut the fruit in half following the natural indentation, then cut out the stone with a knife.

chutney is thick and there is no free liquid.

Ladle the chutney into warm, clean, dry jars taking care not to trap any air bubbles. Cover with vinegar-proof lids and seal (see pages 12-13). Store in a cool, dark, dry place for 2 months before eating.

Fresh Date and Orange Chutney

The date palm was the tree of life in the Garden of Eden, and it is said to have over 800 uses. There is even an Arab belief that, when Allah created the world, he formed the date palm not from common clay but from the material remaining after he had built Adam.

MAKES ABOUT 1.4KG/3LB

450g/1lb oranges
675g/1½lb fresh dates, stoned and finely chopped
450g/1lb onions, finely chopped
3 garlic cloves, finely chopped
115g/4oz dried apricots, chopped
115g/4oz raisins
750g/1lb 10oz soft light brown sugar
good pinch of cayenne pepper
2 tablespoons sea salt
1.3 litres/2¼ pints white wine vinegar

Grate the zest from the oranges then, working over a bowl, peel off and discard the white pith from the fruit. Chop the flesh in a saucepan so as not to waste any juice; discard the pips. Add any juice collected in the bowl, half the orange zest and all the remaining ingredients to the pan and heat gently, stirring, until the sugar has dissolved. Raise the heat and bring to the boil, then simmer gently for about 1 hour, stirring occasionally, until thick and there is no free liquid. Stir in the remaining orange zest.

Spoon into warm, clean, dry jars taking

care not to trap any air bubbles. Cover and seal (see pages 12-13). Store in a cool, dark, dry place for 4-6 weeks before eating.

Fresh Date and Pineapple Chutney

The original version I have of this recipe comes from before the Second World War, so it called for dried dates and canned pineapple. That chutney was quite good but not particularly special. However, if you use fresh dates and pineapples, which are now readily available, the chutney is transformed.

MAKES ABOUT 2KG/4½LB

225g/8oz onions, chopped
1 pineapple, weighing about 1.4kg/3lb, peeled, cored and cut into small pieces
450g/1lb cooking apples, peeled, cored and chopped
1 teaspoon ground cinnamon
425ml/15fl oz cider vinegar
225g/8oz fresh dates, stoned and coarsely chopped
225g/8oz warmed soft light brown sugar (see page 7)

Gently simmer the onions, pineapple, apples, cinnamon and vinegar for 30-40 minutes until the fruit is soft.

Stir in the dates and warmed sugar until it has dissolved, then bring slowly to the boil and boil gently for 20-25 minutes, stirring frequently, until the fruit is well coated in thick syrup.

Ladle the chutney into warm, clean, dry jars, making sure that you do not trap any air bubbles. Cover the jars with vinegar-proof lids and seal (see pages 12-13). Store in a cool, dark, dry place for 2 months before eating.

$\mathcal{M}$ANGOES, $\mathcal{G}$UAVAS

Mango Butter

Shortly before the butter is ready, taste it to see if the cardamom flavour is strong enough; if it is not, toast and crush a few more seeds to stir in. Alternatively, have some more prepared just in case.

MAKES ABOUT 1.1KG/2½LB

1 teaspoon cardamom seeds
900g/2lb firm but ripe mangoes, peeled
115ml/4fl oz lemon juice
115ml/4fl oz orange juice
800g/1¾lb warmed sugar (see page 7)

Heat the cardamom seeds in a small, dry, heavy-based frying pan until fragrant, moving them gently around the pan to prevent them from catching. Remove the seeds from the pan and crush them using a mortar and pestle or in a small blender; set aside.

Cut the mango flesh from the stones, then chop it and put in a pan with the lemon and orange juices. Bring to the boil, then simmer, stirring occasionally, until the mangoes are soft and there is no free liquid.

Pass the mangoes through a vegetable mill or press through a fine non-metallic sieve with a wooden spoon and return to the rinsed pan. Over a low heat, stir in the warmed sugar and the cardamom seeds and heat gently, stirring, until the sugar has dissolved. Boil, stirring occasionally at first, then increasingly frequently, until the mixture has the consistency of thick double cream. This should take 30-45 minutes.

Spoon the butter into warm, clean, dry pots. Cover and seal (see pages 12-13). Store in a cool, dark, dry place for a few days before eating.

Serve for breakfast with toasted brioche or warmed croissants.

Guava Jelly

Slightly under-ripe guavas work best in this recipe. If getting a set is a problem, use sugar with pectin.

MAKES ABOUT 675G/1½LB

1.4kg/3lb guavas, thinly sliced
3 cardamom pods, crushed (optional)
675g/1½lb warmed sugar
 (see page 7)
juice of 1-2 large lemons, depending on the
 acidity of the guavas

Put the guavas and cardamom pods, if used, into a pan, add water to barely cover and bring to the boil, then simmer for about 45 minutes until the fruit is very soft.

Purée the fruit by passing it through a non-

Above: Mango Butter makes a glamorous and exotically flavoured spread.

metallic sieve or blending it, then tip it into a scalded jelly bag suspended over a non-metallic bowl and leave in a cool place to strain, undisturbed, for 8-12 hours.

Measure the strained juice and pour it into the pan. Add 450g/1lb sugar for 570ml/1 pint juice. Add the lemon juice and heat gently, stirring, until the sugar has dissolved. Raise the heat and boil hard for 10-15 minutes until setting point is reached (see page 17).

Remove from the heat and skim the scum from the surface with a slotted spoon. Ladle into warm, clean, dry jars. Cover and seal (see pages 12-13). Leave overnight to set. Store in a cool, dark, dry place.

 DRIED FRUITS

Shiny black, plump Prunes in Armagnac (see page 114); deep, glowing, amber-coloured Dried Apricot and Benedictine Conserve (see page 112); chunky chutneys and spicy piquant pickles can all be prepared inexpensively at any time of the year using a wide variety of dried fruits. An added bonus of using dried fruits is that they rarely need any preparation other than an initial soaking. For the best results, try to find fruit that has been dried naturally in the sun and choose fruits that have not been treated with preservatives such as sulphur dioxide and mineral oils.

Left (from left to right): Spiced Dried Fruits, Dried Apricot and Pear Jam, Dried Apricot and Orange Mincemeat.

Dried Apricot and Benedictine Conserve

Sufferers from rheumatism have a very good excuse for eating generous amounts of this richly flavoured preserve as Benedictine is reputed to ease such complaints.

MAKES ABOUT 2KG/4½LB

450g/1lb dried apricots
warmed sugar (see page 7)
grated zest and juice of 1 orange
50g/2oz flaked almonds
4 tablespoons Benedictine

Put the apricots and 1.2 litres/2 pints water in a non-metallic bowl and leave to soak overnight.

Tip the contents of the bowl into a pan and bring to simmering point, then cover and cook gently for about 45 minutes until the apricots are very soft.

Purée the apricots by pressing through a non-metallic sieve or blending. Measure the purée and return to the pan with 450g/1lb sugar to each 570ml/1 pint purée. Stir in the orange zest and juice and bring to the boil, then boil for about 10 minutes, stirring as necessary, until thick.

Remove from the heat and stir in the almonds and Benedictine. Leave to stand for 10-15 minutes, then stir and ladle into warm, clean, dry jars. Cover and seal (see pages 12-13). Leave overnight to set. Store in a cool, dark, dry place.

Hunza Apricot Honey

Hunza apricots can be found in good health food shops and will repay the search. They have a wonderful flavour and, reputedly, they have profound health-giving properties.

MAKES ABOUT 850ML-1 LITRE/1½-1¾ PINTS

900g/2lb hunza apricots
2 tablespoons lemon juice
175g/6oz clear honey

Put the apricots in a non-metallic bowl, pour over 850ml/1½ pints boiling water and leave to soak for about 4 hours.

Drain the apricots, saving the soaking liquid. Boil the liquid for 15-20 minutes until reduced to 425ml/15fl oz.

Meanwhile, stone and coarsely chop the apricots. Add to the reduced liquid with the lemon juice and simmer until the fruit is soft.

Tip the contents of the pan into a non-metallic sieve placed over a non-metallic bowl. Press firmly with a wooden spoon on the contents of the sieve to force through as much as possible. Return the purée to the pan, then stir in the honey and cook, stirring as necessary, until a clear trail is left on the bottom of the pan when the spoon is drawn through the mixture.

Spoon the honey into warm, clean, dry pots. Cover and seal (see pages 12-13). Store in a cool, dark, dry place.

Dried Apricot, Apple and Cider Jam

MAKES ABOUT 2.2KG/5LB

225g/8oz dried apricots, chopped
570ml/1 pint dry cider
900g/2lb cooking apples, peeled, cored
 and chopped
1½ tablespoons lemon juice
1.4kg/3lb warmed sugar (see page 7)

Put the apricots into a non-metallic bowl, add the cider and leave to soak overnight.

Tip the contents of the bowl into a pan, add the apples and bring to the boil. Lower the heat and simmer for about 1 hour until the fruit is soft and pulpy.

Over a low heat, stir in the lemon juice and warmed sugar until the sugar has dissolved, then raise the heat and boil hard for 10-15 minutes, stirring as necessary, until setting point is reached (see page 17).

Remove from the heat and skim the scum from the surface with a slotted spoon. Ladle into warm, clean, dry jars. Cover and seal (see pages 12-13). Leave overnight to set. Store in a cool, dark, dry place.

Left (clockwise from top centre): dried prunes, peaches, hunza apricots, apricots, figs, apples, pears, dates and mango strips.

*A*PRICOTS

Dried Apricot and Orange Mincemeat

Carrots keep this unusual mincemeat nice and moist, while cardamom adds a subtle complementary note.

MAKES ABOUT 1.1KG/2½LB

225g/8oz dried apricots, chopped
finely grated zest and juice of 2 large oranges
finely grated zest and juice of 1 lime
225g/8oz sultanas
115g/4oz raisins, chopped
75g/3oz mixed peel
115g/4oz flaked almonds
115g/4oz soft dark brown sugar
225g/8oz carrots, grated
150g/5oz shredded vegetarian or beef suet
seeds from 6 cardamom pods, finely crushed
1½ teaspoons ground cinnamon
½ teaspoon grated nutmeg
4 tablespoons Cointreau
150ml/5fl oz whisky

Thoroughly stir all the ingredients together in a large non-metallic bowl, then cover and leave in a cool place overnight or for at least 8 hours, stirring occasionally.

Pack the mincemeat tightly into clean, dry jars, taking care not to leave any air pockets. Cover and seal (see pages 12-13). Store in a cool, dark, dry place for at least 1 month before eating.

Mincemeat Pudding

SERVES 4

75g/3oz unsalted butter, softened
65g/2½oz soft dark brown sugar
2 eggs, size 3, beaten
115g/4oz self-raising flour
225g/8oz Dried Apricot and Orange Mincemeat
 (see above)
real custard or vanilla dairy ice cream, to serve

Preheat the oven to 160°C/325°F/gas mark 3 and butter a 20cm/8in shallow, round ovenproof dish.

In a bowl, beat together the butter and sugar until light and fluffy, then gradually beat in the eggs, beating well after each addition. Using a large metal spoon, gently fold in the flour, followed by the mincemeat.

Spoon the mixture into the dish and bake

Above: home-made mincemeat provides the basis for a delicious and speedy Mincemeat Pudding.

for 10 minutes. Lower the oven temperature to 150°C/300°F/gas mark 2 and bake for a further 40-45 minutes or until a knife inserted in the centre comes out clean. Serve this sensational pudding hot with real custard or vanilla dairy ice cream.

Dried Apricot and Pear Jam

Dried apricots and pears give a well-flavoured jam, and they really come into their own for making jam in the winter when fresh fruit is scarce and expensive. The apricot kernels add an almond flavour as well as an interesting crunch.

MAKES ABOUT 2.2KG/4¾LB

450g/1lb hunza apricots
450g/1lb dried pears
1 vanilla pod
1 cinnamon stick
grated zest and juice of 2 lemons
warmed sugar (see page 7)

Soak the apricots for several hours in 1.2 litres/2 pints water. Drain the apricots, reserving the liquid.

Put the pears, vanilla, cinnamon, lemon zest and juice, 900ml/1½ pints water and the reserved liquid in a pan, bring to the boil, then reduce the heat and simmer for about 10 minutes, stirring occasionally, until the pears are tender.

Remove the stones from the apricots and crack them with nutcrackers, a rolling pin or a hammer to remove the kernels.

Over a low heat, stir the warmed sugar and apricots into the pan until the sugar has dissolved. Raise the heat and boil for about 20 minutes, stirring frequently, until setting point is reached (see page 17). Remove the vanilla pod and cinnamon stick.

Remove from the heat and leave for about 15 minutes. Stir in the kernels, then ladle into warm, clean, dry jars. Cover and seal (see pages 12-13). Leave overnight to set. Store in a cool, dark, dry place.

Variation: *Dried Apricot and Hazelnut Jam*
Soak 450g/1lb dried apricots in 1.7 litres/ 3 pints water overnight, then cook in the water and juice of 1 large lemon until soft.

Over a low heat, stir in 1.4kg/3lb sugar until dissolved. Continue as above, adding 50g/2oz toasted and chopped hazelnuts instead of the apricot kernels. Makes about 2.2kg/5lb.

Dried Peach and Chestnut Chutney

I have used cooked chestnuts for this chunky, nutty chutney but chopped walnuts, almonds or hazelnuts can easily be substituted.

MAKES ABOUT 1.8KG/4LB

450g/1lb dried peaches
450g/1lb onions, chopped
finely grated zest and juice of 2 large oranges
225g/8oz raisins
1 garlic clove, chopped
1 teaspoon English mustard powder
½ teaspoon ground allspice
450g/1lb soft light brown sugar
850ml/1½ pints cider vinegar
225g/8oz cooked chestnuts, quartered

Place the peaches in a non-metallic bowl and pour in cold water just to cover them.

The next day, drain the peaches, reserving the liquid, then chop them. Pour the liquid into a pan and boil until well reduced. Stir in the remaining ingredients, except the chestnuts, and bring to the boil. Lower the heat and simmer for 1 hour, stirring frequently, until the mixture is thick and jam-like and there is no free liquid.

Remove the pan from the heat and stir in the nuts, then ladle the chutney into warm, clean, dry jars, pressing down to expel any air. Cover with vinegar-proof lids and seal (see pages 12-13). Store in a cool, dark, dry place for at least 1 month before eating.

Prunes in Armagnac

As well as being a good way of making the most of good-quality prunes, this is excellent for improving inferior ones. Dry the orange peel in an oven set to its lowest temperature. When choosing a jar, don't forget that the prunes will swell during storage.

MAKES ABOUT 1 LITRE/1¾ PINTS

450g/1lb plump prunes
425ml/15fl oz freshly made, hot, fragrant tea, such as orange Pekoe or Earl Grey
1 strip dried orange peel
225ml/8fl oz Armagnac
115g/4oz soft brown sugar

Place the prunes and tea in a pan and bring to the boil, then simmer for 3 minutes and remove from the heat. Strain off and reserve the liquid.

Pack the prunes into a clean, dry, jar, inserting the orange peel at the same time. Pour in the Armagnac.

Return the reserved liquid to the pan, add the sugar and heat gently, stirring, until it has dissolved. Raise the heat and bring to the boil, then simmer until syrupy. Pour into the jar so the prunes are well covered.

Swivel the jar to expel any air then cover tightly. Leave in a cool, dark, dry place for up to 2 months, shaking the jar occasionally, before eating.

Serve with roast pork or game; dilute the juice slightly and use to deglaze a pan after frying pork steaks, and serve along with some of the prunes; use as a simple dessert accompanied by ice cream; eat both chilled prunes and juice with a crisp almond biscuit; add to fruit salads.

Variation: *Prunes in Rum*
Replace the Armagnac with rum and proceed as above. Makes about 1 litre/ 1¾ pints.

$\mathscr{P}$RUNES

Prune, Dried Fruit and Pecan Compôte

A few jars of this compôte will come in handy during the winter for quick or impromptu puddings, or will add a taste of luxury to plain ones. If you want a less spicy mixture, put all the spices in a muslin bag then discard this after the soaking.

MAKES ABOUT 2 LITRES/3½ PINTS

1 bottle red wine
1 bay leaf
4 cloves
1 cinnamon stick
2 star anise
1 vanilla pod
½ teaspoon coriander seeds
5 black peppercorns
350g/12oz prunes, stoned
750g/22oz mixed dried apricots, peaches,
 pears and figs, coarsely chopped
50g/2oz pecans
250g/9oz sugar
4 tablespoons brandy

Simmer the wine with the spices for 30 minutes. Pour over the fruit in a non-metallic bowl and leave to soak overnight.

Using a slotted spoon, pack the fruit into clean, dry heatproof jars with the spices, if retaining. Put the nuts in amongst the fruit.

Pour the wine into a pan, add the sugar and heat gently, stirring, until the sugar has dissolved. Raise the heat and boil until syrupy. Remove from the heat, add the brandy and ladle into the jars. Swivel the jars to expel any air. Cover and seal (see pages 12–13). Store in a cool, dark, dry place for 3-4 weeks before eating.

Left: Prune, Dried Fruit and Pecan Compôte, a deliciously nutty and textured preserve.

Prune and Raisin Conserve

MAKES ABOUT 1.6KG/3½LB

570g/1¼lb prunes, halved and stoned
350g/12oz raisins
115g/4oz dried figs or stoned dried dates,
 chopped
500ml/18fl oz freshly made, hot Earl Grey tea
finely grated zest and juice of 1 orange
juice of 1 lemon
2 cloves
225g/8oz soft dark brown sugar, warmed
 (see page 7)
50g/2oz walnut halves
4 tablespoons kirsch or dark rum

Put all the dried fruits into a bowl, pour over
the tea, cover and leave overnight.

Tip the contents of the bowl into a pan,
add the remaining ingredients, except the
nuts and kirsch or rum, and heat gently,
stirring, until the sugar has dissolved. Raise
the heat and bring to the boil, then simmer
for about 12 minutes, stirring, until a light
setting point is reached (see page 17).

Remove the pan from the heat, add the
nuts and kirsch or rum and ladle into warm,
clean, dry jars. Cover and seal (see pages
12-13). Store in a cool, dark, dry place for
several days before eating.

Spiced Prunes

MAKES ABOUT 700ML/1¼ PINTS

450g/1lb plump prunes
450ml/15fl oz freshly made, hot Earl Grey tea
115g/4oz sugar
1 teaspoon cloves
8 allspice berries
1 blade of mace
2.5cm/1in piece of cinnamon stick
150ml/5fl oz white wine vinegar
few short strips of orange zest

Soak the prunes in the tea in a covered non-
metallic bowl overnight.

The next day, place the sugar, spices and
the vinegar in a pan and heat gently, stirring,
until the sugar has dissolved, then raise the
heat and boil for 5 minutes. Add the prunes
and their soaking liquid, cover and simmer
gently for about 20 minutes, until tender.

Using a slotted spoon, pack the prunes
firmly into a warm, clean, dry jar, pushing
some short strips of orange zest among the
fruit. Bring the liquid to the boil, then pour it
over the prunes. Swivel the jar to dispel any
air bubbles. Cover with vinegar-proof lids
and seal (see pages 12-13). Store in a cool,
dark, dry place for 1 month before eating.

———— ⤴ ————

Serve with ham, pork, goose or hare; braise
with red cabbage; use a little of the juice to
deglaze the juices of roast or fried meats.

Dried Fruit Chutney

You can either chop the dried fruits coarsely
for a chunky chutney, or finely for a
smoother one.

MAKES ABOUT 2.2KG/5LB

225g/8oz dried peaches, chopped
225g/8oz dried apricots, chopped
225g/8oz dried pears, chopped
570ml/1 pint white wine vinegar
450g/1lb cooking apples, preferably Bramleys,
 peeled, cored and chopped
225g/8oz onions, finely chopped
2 garlic cloves, finely chopped
115g/4oz raisins
½ teaspoon ground coriander
½ teaspoon ground cloves
1 teaspoon English mustard powder
good pinch of cayenne pepper
1 teaspoon sea salt
675g/1½lb soft light brown sugar, warmed
 (see page 7)

Leave the dried peaches, apricots and pears
to soak in the vinegar in a non-metallic bowl
overnight.

The next day, tip the contents of the bowl
into a pan and bring to the boil, then add the
remaining ingredients, except for the sugar,
and simmer for 30 minutes until all the fruits
are tender.

Over a low heat, stir in the warmed sugar
until it has dissolved. Raise the heat and
boil, stirring frequently, for 15-20 minutes,
until the ingredients are tender and the
chutney is thick and there is no free liquid.

Spoon into warm, clean, dry jars, taking
care not to leave any air bubbles. Cover with
vinegar-proof lids and seal (see pages 12-
13). Store in a cool, dark, dry place for at
least 2 months before eating.

Spiced Dried Fruits

These are sweet enough to serve for
dessert (you can add a little sugar if they
are not sweet enough for your taste), yet
they can also be served with meats or
added to pork, lamb, pheasant or partridge
casseroles (see page 117).

MAKES ABOUT 1.4KG/3LB

900g/2lb mixed dried fruit, such as prunes,
 apple rings, pears, peaches, apricots
5cm/2in piece of fresh ginger, grated
2 teaspoons each allspice berries and cloves
1 cinnamon stick
pared zest of 1 lemon
400ml/14fl oz cider vinegar
400g/14oz sugar

Put all the dried fruit in a non-metallic bowl,
cover it with water and leave to soak
overnight.

Place the spices, lemon zest and vinegar
in a pan and bring to the boil, then simmer
for 10 minutes. Leave to cool.

Meanwhile, pour the dried fruits and their

soaking liquid into a pan and simmer gently, covered, until tender.

Strain the vinegar through a non-metallic sieve lined with muslin, then return it to the pan. Add the sugar and heat gently, stirring, until it has dissolved. Raise the heat and bring to the boil, then simmer for 7-10 minutes until syrupy.

Drain the fruits and pack into warm, clean, dry jars. Pour in the hot vinegar to cover completely. Swivel the jars to expel any air. Cover with vinegar-proof lids and seal (see pages 12-13). Store in a cool, dark, dry place for at least 1 month before eating.

Braised Lamb with Spiced Dried Fruits

This can be cooked one day in advance up to when the dried fruits are added, to allow the flavours to develop. The next day, about 30 minutes before serving, I bring the casserole slowly to the boil, cover and simmer gently for about 20 minutes, adding the fruits halfway through cooking.

SERVES 4

675g/1½lb boned leg of lamb, cubed
1½ tablespoons mild olive oil
1 onion, finely chopped
1 garlic clove, finely chopped
2 teaspoons plain flour
1 cinnamon stick
1 teaspoon ground allspice
450ml/15fl oz stock
finely grated zest and juice of 1 orange
finely grated zest and juice of ½ lemon
100ml/3½fl oz spiced vinegar from the
  Spiced Dried Fruits (see page 116)
about 1 tablespoon clear honey
pinch of cayenne pepper
salt and freshly ground black pepper
about 10 pieces of Spiced Dried Fruit,
  halved if large

Preheat the oven to 170°C/325°F/gas mark 3.

Brown the lamb in batches in the oil in a heavy flameproof casserole; remove with a slotted spoon and reserve.

Stir the onion into the casserole, cook gently until soft, adding the garlic towards the end. Stir in the flour and spices for 1 minute then stir in the stock, fruit zests and

Above: Braised Lamb with Spiced Dried Fruits is a sumptuously rich, sweet-sour casserole.

juice, spiced vinegar, honey, cayenne and seasoning. Bring to the boil, stirring.

Return the lamb to the casserole, cover tightly and cook for 1 hour and 10 minutes. Stir in the spiced dried fruits, cover and cook for a further 10 minutes or until tender.

Dates, Figs, Mangoes

Low-sugar Date and Apricot Jam

The concentrated natural sugar in the dried fruits means that little additional sugar is needed in this jam. It is not sufficiently low in overall sugar, however, to be suitable for diabetics.

MAKES ABOUT 1.1KG/2½LB

450g/1lb dried apricots
675g/1½lb dried dates, pitted and chopped
225g/8oz warmed sugar (see page 7)
juice of 1 lemon
50g/2oz hazelnuts, chopped

Put the apricots in a non-metallic bowl, add 570ml/1 pint water, cover and leave to stand for 12 hours, or overnight, until the apricots are plump.

Tip the contents of the bowl into a pan, add an additional 570ml/1 pint water and the dates and simmer until the apricots are soft and tender.

Over a low heat, add the warmed sugar and the lemon juice and stir until the sugar has dissolved. Raise the heat and bring to the boil, then reduce the heat and simmer, stirring occasionally, until the jam thickens. Add the hazelnuts and simmer for a further 2 minutes.

Remove the pan from the heat and skim off any scum that has formed on the surface with a slotted spoon. Leave the jam to cool for 10-15 minutes, then stir and ladle the jam into warm, clean, dry jars. Cover and seal (see pages 12-13). Leave to cool, then store in a cool, dark, dry place for a few days before eating.

Variations: use walnuts or almonds instead of hazelnuts; use the juice of an orange instead of a lemon.

Dried Fig and Apple Jam

The fruit in this recipe can either be chopped by hand (I chop both fruits together) or it can be put through a mincer. If you would prefer to remove the fig seeds, press the cooked fruit through a non-metallic sieve (if you do this, there is no need to peel and core the apples).

MAKES ABOUT 1.8KG/4LB

1.4kg/3lb apples, peeled, cored and finely chopped
450g/1lb dried figs, stalks removed, finely chopped
finely grated zest and juice of 1 large orange
¼ teaspoon ground cinnamon
¼ teaspoon freshly grated nutmeg
pinch of ground cloves
1.1kg/2½lb warmed sugar (see page 7)

Put all the ingredients, except the sugar, in a pan and just cover with water. Bring to the boil, then simmer for 20-30 minutes, until the fruit is completely tender and the liquid well reduced.

Over a low heat, add the warmed sugar to the pan and stir the mixture until the sugar has dissolved, then raise the heat and boil for 10-15 minutes, stirring as necessary, until setting point is reached (see page 17).

Remove the pan from the heat and skim the scum from the surface using a slotted spoon. Ladle the jam into warm, clean, dry jars. Cover and seal the jars (see pages 12-13). Leave the jars to cool, then store the jam in a cool, dark, dry place for a few days before eating.

Variation: use ground allspice or Chinese five-spice powder instead of cinnamon.

Raisin, Date and Orange Chutney

MAKES ABOUT 1.4KG/3LB

450g/1lb oranges
675g/1½lb dried dates, stoned and chopped
225g/8oz plump raisins
450g/1lb onions, chopped
625g/1lb 6oz sugar
1.4 litres/2½ pints Spiced Vinegar (see page 139)

Finely grate the orange zest and put half into a pan. Remove and discard the orange pith. Chop the oranges, discarding the pips. Add the oranges and remaining ingredients (except the orange zest) to the pan.

Bring the mixture to the boil, then simmer for about 1 hour, stirring occasionally, until the chutney has thickened and no free liquid is visible.

Stir in the remaining orange zest and ladle the chutney into warm, clean, dry jars, taking care not to trap any air bubbles. Cover with vinegar-proof lids and seal (see pages 12-13). Store in a cool, dark, dry place for at least 2 months before eating.

Dried Mango Chutney

Cooked dried mangoes have a more pronounced mango flavour than cooked fresh ones and so make a fruitier chutney.

MAKES ABOUT 1.4KG/3LB

225g/8oz dried mangoes
1 dried red chilli, halved
6 cardamom pods, crushed
3 cloves
5 allspice berries
1 teaspoon coriander seeds, crushed
1 cinnamon stick, broken in half
350g/12oz cooking apples, peeled, cored and chopped

1 garlic clove, cut into slivers
sea salt
300ml/10fl oz white wine vinegar
350g/12oz warmed sugar (see page 7)

Place the mangoes in a non-metallic bowl, just cover them with water and leave to soak overnight. Drain off the soaking liquid and boil until reduced to 300ml/10fl oz.

Gently heat the chilli and spices in a dry heavy-based frying pan until fragrant, moving them around gently so they do not catch, then add to the pan along with the apples, mangoes, garlic, a good pinch of salt and the vinegar. Bring to the boil, then simmer for about 10 minutes, stirring occasionally.

Over a low heat, stir in the warmed sugar until it has dissolved. Raise the heat and boil, stirring frequently, until the chutney is thick and no free liquid is visible.

Spoon the chutney into warm, clean, dry jars, taking care not to trap any air bubbles. Cover with vinegar-proof lids and seal (see pages 12-13). Store in a cool, dark, dry place for 1 month before eating.

Mostarda di Frutta

This is a tongue-tingling combination of sweet and hot rather than sweet and sour.

MAKES ABOUT 600G/1¼LB

115g/4oz English mustard powder
115g/4oz soft light brown sugar
175ml/6fl oz white wine vinegar
115g/4oz each dried apricots, dried figs, raisins
 and glacé cherries, coarsely chopped
50g/2oz dried apple rings, quartered
6 pieces of stem ginger
1 teaspoon sea salt

In a bowl, stir 300ml/10fl oz water into the mustard. Cover and leave for at least 1 hour.

Place the sugar and vinegar in a saucepan and heat gently, stirring, until the sugar has dissolved. Raise the heat to moderate and boil until the mixture begins to thicken.

Stir in the fruits, ginger, mustard and salt and return to the boil, stirring. Simmer until the mixture is quite thick. Leave to cool, then spoon into clean, dry jars; do not trap any air bubbles. Cover with vinegar-proof lids and seal (see pages 12-13). Store in a cool, dark, dry place for 6-8 weeks before eating.

In Lombardy, Mostarda di Frutta is the classic accompaniment to boiled meats, but I suggest you serve it with grilled and roast poultry and meats.

Below: Mostarda di Frutta is an unusual traditional preserve from Lombardy in Italy.

$\mathcal{N}$UTS

As well as adding flavour to numerous sweet and savoury preserves, nuts also provide an interesting texture. Nuts can be the main constituent of a preserve, such as the chestnuts in Chestnut, Vanilla and Rum Jam (see page 122) or they may play a complementary role with other ingredients in recipes such as Pistachio and Pear Conserve (see page 124) and Plum and Orange Jam with Hazelnuts (see page 124). For a more exotic preserve, try Caribbean Jam or Coconut Relish (see page 124). Make sure you use nuts that are as fresh as possible (it is always best to buy them in the shell if you can, as they keep better that way). Even the slightest stale taste in the nuts before they are preserved will be magnified after cooking and spoil the final results.

Left (from left to right): Almond, Carrot and Ginger Chutney, Chestnuts in Syrup and Plum and Orange Jam with Hazelnuts.

Almond, Carrot and Ginger Chutney

The carrots can be grated lengthways, across or on the diagonal, depending on how long you like the strands to be.

MAKES ABOUT 1.1KG/2½LB

450g/1lb carrots, grated
15g/½oz ground coriander
15g/½oz sea salt
generous pinch of cayenne pepper
finely grated zest and juice of 1 lemon
250ml/9fl oz cider vinegar
50g/2oz fresh ginger
350g/12oz warmed sugar (see page 7)
50ml/2fl oz clear honey
generous 25g/1oz flaked almonds

Put the carrots, coriander, salt, cayenne pepper, lemon zest and juice and vinegar into a non-metallic bowl. Grate half the ginger and cut the other half into matchsticks. Stir all the ginger into the bowl, then cover and leave in a cool place overnight.

Tip the contents of the bowl into a pan. Add 150ml/5fl oz water and bring to the boil, then simmer for 20 minutes. Over a low heat, stir in the warmed sugar and honey until both have dissolved, then return to the boil. Simmer for a further 20-25 minutes, stirring as necessary, until the mixture is thick and no free liquid is visible. Stir in the almonds and simmer the mixture for another 4 minutes or so.

Remove the chutney from the heat and ladle into warm, clean, dry jars, taking care not to trap any air bubbles. Cover with vinegar-proof lids and seal (see pages 12-13). Allow to mature for at least a few days, preferably much longer, before eating.

Chestnuts in Syrup

Peeling chestnuts is a laborious task but don't be tempted to use reconstituted dried chestnuts. You will be so disappointed with the end result that you will have wasted your time. You need to end up with 350g/12oz prepared nuts. Glucose can be bought from a chemist's shop.

MAKES ABOUT 350G/12OZ

about 600-675g/1¼-1½lb chestnuts
1 vanilla pod
225g/8oz sugar
225g/8oz liquid glucose
2 tablespoons brandy or dark rum (optional)

Make a slit in the skin of each chestnut, then add them to a pan of boiling water and simmer for 10 minutes. Remove the pan from the heat and, using a slotted spoon, remove the nuts, one by one. When they are cool enough to handle, remove both the tough outer skin and the fine inner one (see below).

Simmer the chestnuts and vanilla pod in just enough water to cover for about 5 minutes or until tender but not breaking up. Drain and dry on paper towels; reserve the vanilla pod.

Peeling chestnuts: when preparing chestnuts, be sure to remove the fine inner skin as well as the tough outer shell.

Gently heat the sugar, glucose and 175ml/6fl oz water in a pan large enough to hold the chestnuts, stirring until the sugar and glucose have dissolved. Raise the heat and bring to the boil. Remove from the heat and add the chestnuts, then return to the boil. Take off the heat again, then cover and leave overnight.

The next day, uncover the pan and boil the chestnuts in the syrup once more. Remove the pan from the heat, cover and once more leave overnight. The following day, add the vanilla pod and boil for the last time. Off the heat, stir in the brandy or dark rum, if used, then pour the chestnuts and syrup into a warm, clean, dry jar. Swivel the jar to expel any air bubbles. Cover and seal (see pages 12-13). Store in a cool, dark, dry place.

———— 🥄 ————

Serve for dessert with crème fraîche, ice cream or Greek yogurt; serve with chocolate soufflés or other chocolate desserts, or chocolate cake; serve with crème caramel or vanilla bavarois.

Chestnut, Vanilla and Rum Jam

This is a superior version of *crème de marrons* that is sold in small pots. I like to use light soft brown sugar for this recipe.

MAKES ABOUT 1.4KG/3LB

about 1.25kg/2¾lb chestnuts
1 vanilla pod
600g/1¼lb light soft brown sugar, warmed (see page 7)
2 tablespoons dark rum

Prepare the chestnuts as for Chestnuts in Syrup (see left).

Put the nuts and vanilla pod in a saucepan and add just enough water to cover. Cover

$\mathcal{C}$HESTNUTS

the pan and bring to the boil, then simmer for about 30 minutes until the chestnuts are tender. Drain the chestnuts, reserving the liquid. Remove the vanilla pod from the chestnuts then pass the nuts through a vegetable mill or purée in a blender or food processor. Weigh the purée; there should be about 750g/1lb 10oz.

Split the vanilla pod lengthways and scrape out the seeds. Put the pod and seeds in a heavy-based pan, add the chestnut purée, the sugar and 100ml/3½fl oz reserved cooking liquid. Heat gently, stirring until the sugar has dissolved, then boil until the mixture is thick. Discard the vanilla pod and stir in the rum.

Spoon the jam into warm, clean, dry jars, cover and seal (see pages 12-13). Leave overnight to cool and set slightly. This delicious jam will keep for about 6 months in a cool, dark, dry place.

Use to sandwich chocolate cakes together, or to fill a chocolate Swiss roll; spoon into meringue baskets, top with a swirl of cream and decorate with plenty of dark chocolate shavings; fill chocolate pancakes; stir into crème anglaise, crème pâtissière or whipped cream; use as the base for soufflés, mousses and ice creams; mix with whipped cream, crème fraîche or yogurt to make a quick chestnut fool (see right); serve with lightly sweetened poached orange slices or kumquats.

Right: use Chestnut, Vanilla and Rum Jam layered with cream, crème fraîche or Greek yogurt to make a delicious chestnut fool.

Caribbean Jam

An exotic jam to make for special occasions or special people.

MAKES ABOUT 1.4KG/3LB

1 coconut
6 limes
1 pineapple
2 cooking apples, chopped but not peeled
 or cored
900g/2lb warmed sugar (see page 7)

Pierce the eyes of the coconut with a meat skewer and drain the liquid into a pan. Crack open the coconut with a hammer and cut the flesh away from the shell. Coarsely grate the flesh and add it to the pan. Grate the lime zest and set aside. Squeeze the juice from the limes (reserve the shells) and add to the pan. Chop the lime shells and put these in the pan.

Peel the pineapple, making sure you remove all the eyes. Chop the flesh quite finely and mix this with the lime zest. Chop the pineapple peel and put into the pan with the apples and 1.4 litres/2 pints water. Bring to the boil, then cover and simmer steadily for about 1 hour.

Strain the boiled juice into a clean pan, pressing down well on the peels. Add the pineapple flesh and lime zest to the pan and simmer for about 20 minutes, stirring occasionally, until the pineapple is tender.

Over a low heat, stir in the warmed sugar until it has dissolved. Raise the heat and boil hard for 10-15 minutes, stirring as necessary, until setting point is reached (see page 17).

Remove the pan from the heat and skim the surface with a slotted spoon. Ladle the jam into warm, clean, dry jars. Cover and seal (see pages 12-13). Leave overnight to set. Store in a cool, dark, dry place.

———— ⟿ ————

Delicious with toast or added to plain yogurt.

Coconut Relish

This recipe was given to me by the daughter-in-law of a neighbour. When I told this neighbour I was writing a book on preserving she told me her daughter-in-law had an 'interesting' relish recipe that she would get for me. Unlike many things which are described as 'interesting' because nothing else that isn't derogatory can be said about them, this crunchy pickle is indeed very good.

MAKES ABOUT 675G/1½LB

1 coconut
½ teaspoon ground ginger
1 cinnamon stick
good pinch of cayenne powder
1 large onion (not Spanish), finely chopped
2-3 garlic cloves, chopped
50-115g/2-4oz granulated sugar
1 teaspoon sea salt
300ml/10fl oz cider vinegar

Pierce the eyes of the coconut with a meat skewer and pour the liquid into a pan. Crack open the coconut with a hammer and cut the flesh away from the shell. Coarsely grate the flesh and add it to the pan with the remaining ingredients.

Bring to the boil, stirring, then cover the pan and simmer for 30 minutes. Remove the lid and boil for about 15 minutes, stirring occasionally, until the liquid has reduced and the relish has thickened.

Remove the chutney from the heat and ladle into warm clean, dry jars. Cover with vinegar-proof lids and seal (see pages 12-13). Store in a cool, dark, dry place for at least 1 month before using.

———— ⟿ ————

Serve with curries and other spicy meat, poultry and fish dishes.

Pistachio and Pear Conserve

The delicate flavour of pistachios goes well with the gentle flavour of pears, and the nuts add pretty flecks of green.

MAKES ABOUT 1.4KG/3LB

1kg/2¼lb pears, peeled, cored and cubed
juice of 1 lemon
1.1kg/2½lb warmed sugar (see page 7)
75g/3oz pistachios, coarsely chopped

Put the pears, lemon juice and 300ml/10fl oz water into a pan and bring to the boil. Lower the heat and simmer for 10 minutes until the pears are tender.

Add the sugar to the pan and stir over a low heat until the sugar has dissolved. Raise the heat and boil hard for 15-20 minutes, stirring occasionally, until the mixture has slightly thickened.

Remove the pan from the heat and skim any scum from the surface, then stir in the nuts. Leave to stand for 10-15 minutes, then stir and ladle the conserve into warm, clean, dry jars taking care not to trap any air bubbles. Cover and seal (see pages 12-13). Leave overnight to set slightly. Store in a cool, dark, dry place.

Plum and Orange Jam with Hazelnuts

Lightly toasted chopped hazelnuts add both flavour and texture to this popular jam.

MAKES ABOUT 1.4KG/3LB

1kg/2¼lb plums, stoned
finely grated zest and juice of 1 small orange
 or 1 lime
115g/4oz hazelnuts
1kg/2¼lb sugar

$\mathscr{P}$ECANS

into a colander and rub with a cloth to remove the skins. Chop the nuts. Stir the sugar and nuts into the plums until the sugar has dissolved. Raise the heat and boil hard for 10-15 minutes, stirring as necessary, until setting point is reached (see page 17).

Remove from the heat and skim the scum from the surface with a slotted spoon. Leave to stand for 10-15 minutes, then stir and ladle into warm, clean, dry jars. Cover and seal (see pages 12-13). Leave overnight to set. Store in a cool, dark, dry place.

Pecan and Whisky Mincemeat

A generous measure of whisky adds to the piquancy of this mincemeat as it matures.

MAKES ABOUT 1.1KG/2½LB

115g/4oz pecans, chopped
350g/12oz cooking apples, peeled, cored and
 finely chopped
200g/7oz plump raisins
115g/4oz dried apricots, finely chopped
75g/3oz each stoned dates and dried figs,
 finely chopped
150g/5oz sultanas
1 teaspoon freshly grated nutmeg
1 teaspoon ground cinnamon
pinch of ground allspice
175g/6oz shredded beef or vegetable suet
115g/4oz dark soft brown sugar
finely grated zest and juice of 2 oranges
finely grated zest and juice of 1 lemon
300ml/10fl oz whisky

Put the plums in a pan with 75ml/3fl oz water and the orange or lime juice and zest. Bring to the boil, then simmer for about 20 minutes until the fruit is soft. Meanwhile, preheat the grill. Spread the hazelnuts in a single layer on a baking sheet and toast until

Above: spoonfuls of Pecan and Whisky Mincemeat wrapped inside filo pastry parcels and baked make a simple but delicious end to a meal.

the skins split and the nuts begin to brown; stir as necessary so they brown evenly. Tip

Stir together all the ingredients in a non-metallic bowl. Cover and leave in a cool place for 24 hours, stirring occasionally.

Pack the mincemeat tightly into clean, dry jars, pressing down to expel any air. Cover and seal (see pages 12-13). Store in a cool, dark, dry place for 6-8 weeks before using.

Roast Beef with Pickled Walnut Sauce

Traditional British pickled walnuts seemed to me to be appropriate to serve with equally traditional British roast beef. The slightly piquant, rich flavour of the sauce is a fitting companion for the luxuriousness of a good roast joint.

SERVES 6

1 piece of rib of beef on the bone, weighing
 about 2.2kg/5lb
mild olive oil for brushing
freshly ground black pepper
6 Pickled Walnuts (see left), drained
350ml/12fl oz red wine
about 75ml/3fl oz stock, preferably beef
15g/½oz unsalted butter
salt and pepper

Preheat the oven to 230°C/450°F/gas mark 8. Weigh the meat to calculate the cooking time, then brush with oil and sprinkle with black pepper – do not add salt. Put the joint on a rack in a roasting tin. Roast for 10-12 minutes, then lower the oven temperature to 180°C/350°F/gas mark 4 and cook for 12-15 minutes per 450g/1lb for rare, 15-18 minutes for medium-rare or 18-20 minutes for well-done. Baste the meat occasionally with the cooking juices. Switch off the oven. Transfer the rack with the beef on it to a plate and return to the oven. Prop the door open with the handle of a wooden spoon.

Pour off the surplus fat from the roasting tin, leaving behind the sediment. Add the pickled walnuts into the cooking juices, mashing them with a fork, then stir in the wine. Bring to the boil, then stir in the stock and boil until concentrated to your liking.

Over a low heat, gradually stir in the butter, making sure each piece is incorporated before the next is added. Season and pour into a warm sauceboat to serve with the beef.

Pickled Walnuts

Pick the nuts before the shells have formed; in Britain, this is usually at the end of June.

MAKES ABOUT 2 LITRES/3½ PINTS

450g/1lb green walnuts
115g/4oz table salt
40g/1½oz fresh ginger
1.7 litres/3 pints white wine vinegar
75g/3oz black peppercorns
40g/1½oz allspice berries

Prick the nuts well all over with a darning needle and put them in a non-metallic bowl. Dissolve half the salt in 570ml/1 pint water, pour over the nuts, cover and leave for 1 week to remove any bitterness.

Above: Roast Beef with Pickled Walnut Sauce makes a fine partnership for a special meal.

Drain off and throw away the liquid. Dissolve the remaining salt in a further 570ml/1 pint water, pour over the nuts and leave for a further fortnight.

Drain the walnuts (discarding the liquid), rinse and dry. Spread out the nuts and leave exposed to the air for 2-3 weeks until they have turned black. Pack into clean, dry jars.

Bruise the ginger with the flat of a knife, then place the vinegar and spices in a pan and boil for 10 minutes, pour the liquid over the nuts. Swivel to expel any air bubbles. Leave to cool. Cover with vinegar-proof lids and seal (see pages 12-13). Store in a cool, dark, dry place for 1 month before using.

𝒲ALNUTS

Quinn's Sauce

I wouldn't use up my own home-made pickled walnuts to make this sauce, but it is a good way of using commercial ones. Commercial mushroom ketchup can also be used. This is quite potent so use sparingly.

MAKES ABOUT 570ML/1 PINT

300g/10oz Pickled Walnuts and their liquid
150ml/5fl oz Mushroom Ketchup (see page 31)
3 tablespoons soy sauce
115g/4oz anchovy fillets
12 shallots, finely chopped
1 teaspoon cayenne pepper

Put all the ingredients in a saucepan and bring to the boil, then simmer for 15 minutes. Remove from the heat and leave to cool slightly, then purée in a blender.

Transfer to clean, dry bottles or jars. Cover with vinegar-proof lids and seal (see pages 12-13). Store in a cool dark, dry place for at least 2 weeks before using.

———

This sauce is excellent for making stews and fish sauces; it also good for serving as an accompaniment to fish and all kinds of meat, game and poultry.

Walnut Ketchup

An alternative use for green walnuts is this extremely useful savoury, slightly spicy sauce. The chopping of the nuts can be done in a food processor or blender. Perfectionists strain the nuts through a jelly bag and do not squeeze the bag. The ketchup can then be bottled, in the traditional manner, in a shaker bottle.

MAKES ABOUT 700ML/1¼ PINTS

40 green walnuts, finely chopped
115g/4oz onions, finely chopped
3 blades of mace
6 cloves
1½ teaspoons black peppercorns
1½ teaspoons allspice berries
75g/3oz sea salt
570ml/1 pint white wine vinegar

Put the walnuts in a non-metallic bowl. Put the remaining ingredients in a pan and bring to the boil, then pour over the nuts, cover and leave in a cool place for 2 weeks, stirring daily.

Tip the contents of the bowl into a non-metallic sieve lined with muslin and leave to drain; press on the contents to extract as much juice as possible.

Boil the strained juice in a pan, uncovered, for about 1 hour, then pour into warm, clean, dry bottles. Cover the bottles with vinegar-proof lids and seal (see pages 12-13). Store in a cool, dark, dry place for at least 2-4 weeks before using.

———

Add to soups, casseroles, sauces, marinades and salad dressings; it can also be served as a condiment at the table (a shaker bottle is most convenient for this).

Left: the green walnuts used for Pickled Walnuts and Walnut Ketchup should be picked before the hard shells form.

Walnut Pickle

Chopped nuts make a pickle with an interesting texture. The flavour of the nuts is enhanced by toasting them and adding some walnut oil. Add the grated ginger if you would like a spicier pickle.

MAKES ABOUT 1.1KG/2½LB

450g/1lb walnuts
1 onion, finely chopped
2 garlic cloves, chopped
2 tablespoons mild olive oil
50g/2oz fresh ginger, grated (optional)
1 large cooking apple, peeled, cored
 and chopped
2 tablespoons walnut oil
½-¾ teaspoon freshly grated nutmeg
½ teaspoon paprika
300ml/10fl oz white wine or cider vinegar
175g/6oz sugar

Preheat the grill. Spread the nuts in a single layer in the grill pan and toast them lightly, stirring frequently. Tip on to a chopping board and chop the nuts.

In a pan, gently cook the onion and garlic in the olive oil until soft but not coloured. Stir in the ginger, if using, until fragrant, then add the remaining ingredients. Raise the heat and bring to the boil, then cover and simmer for 15-20 minutes, stirring as necessary.

Ladle the pickle into warm, clean, dry jars. Cover with vinegar-proof lids and seal (see pages 12-13). Store in a cool, dark, dry place for at least 3 weeks before eating.

———

Especially good with all cheeses and dishes containing cheese.

FLOWERS, HERBS AND AROMATICS

The subtle, yet pervasive, scents of flowers, herbs and aromatics give an enticingly unusual taste and aroma to a variety of different preserves. Flowers, herbs and aromatics can be used as the main ingredient of a preserve, such as Elderflower Cordial (see page 130), or they can lend a vital supporting role to other ingredients, adding new life to them, in recipes such as Angelica and Rhubarb Jam (see page 135) as well as in flavoured oils and vinegars (see pages 136-9). Try to avoid using any flowers and herbs that have been treated with chemicals. If you are picking produce from the wild, reject anything that is growing by the roadside. For flowers and herbs in peak condition, pick them in the morning of a dry day after the dew has evaporated but before the sun is hot. Always pick herbs before they have flowered.

Left (from left to right): Herb Oil, Rosehip Syrup, Saffron Garlic, Herb Jelly and Spiced Vinegar.

CARNATIONS, ELDERFLOWERS, ELDERBERRIES

Carnation Liqueur

Of the various carnations, the only one to use for this liqueur is *Dianthus caryophyllus*, the clove pink of old country gardens.

MAKES ABOUT 1 LITRE/1¾ PINTS

150g/5oz carnation heads
1 clove
2.5cm/1in piece of cinnamon stick
570ml/1 pint vodka
225g/8oz sugar

Lightly bruise the carnations with the end of a rolling pin then pack them into a wide-necked bottle with the spices.

Gently warm the vodka in a pan then pour into the bottle. Cover and leave in a warm place for 2 months, shaking the bottle every other day.

Tip the contents of the bottle into a sieve lined with a double thickness of muslin and leave to drain for a few hours.

Gently heat the sugar in 300ml/10fl oz water, stirring until the sugar has dissolved, then leave to cool.

Mix the flavoured vodka with the sugar syrup, then pour into a clean, dry, bottle. Cover and seal (see pages 12-13). This is now ready to drink.

Elderflower Cordial

Making this cordial is a sign that summer has just begun, or should be here very soon. This is really the best way of preserving elderflowers as they turn brown and limp when frozen.

MAKES ABOUT 1.1 LITRES/2 PINTS

about 15 large elderflower umbels (heads)
900g/2lb sugar
1 lemon, sliced
40g/1½oz citric acid
500ml/18fl oz water, boiling

Put the elderflowers, sugar, lemons and citric acid in a large heatproof bowl and stir in the water to dissolve the sugar. Cover and leave in a cool place for 4 days, stirring occasionally; taste to see if the flavour is strong enough, remembering that the cordial will be diluted for drinking.

Strain through a non-metallic sieve lined with muslin and pour into bottles. Seal the bottles (see pages 12-13) and keep in a cool, dark, dry place. This cordial is ready to drink and will keep for a very long time.

Drink chilled, diluted with water or dry white wine; add to fruit desserts such as gooseberry, strawberry, peach or raspberry; use to flavour creamy desserts.

Gooseberry and Elderflower Butter

Gooseberries and luscious muscat-flavoured elderflowers make an ideal partnership. Both are seasonal but, fortuitously, nature has devised that the two seasons coincide. A soft, thick 'buttery' spread, made lightly fragrant by the flowers, is the perfect vehicle for this heavenly combination.

MAKES ABOUT 1.1KG/2½LB

1.4kg/3lb gooseberries
3 elderflower umbels (heads)
warmed sugar (see page 7)

Put the gooseberries, elderflowers and 150ml/5fl oz water in a pan and simmer gently until the fruit is very soft and pulpy.

Push through a non-metallic sieve with a wooden spoon. Measure the purée and return to the rinsed pan with 350g/12oz sugar for every 570ml/1 pint purée.

Add the warmed sugar and heat gently, stirring, until the sugar has dissolved, then increase the heat and boil slowly for about 30-45 minutes, stirring frequently, until the mixture is as thick as double cream.

Spoon into warm, clean, dry jars. Cover and seal (see pages 12-13). Store in a cool, dark, dry place for a few days before eating.

Use to fill a Victoria sandwich cake; fill small, crisp tartlet cases and top with lightly poached gooseberries; or spread on slices of plain cake, scones or not-too-thin slices of freshly cut good-quality white bread.

Elderberry Sauce

Make the most of dark, fragrant elderberries while they are in season by making this delicious, subtly spicy sauce.

MAKES ABOUT 1.1 LITRES/2 PINTS

3 cloves
2 allspice berries
5 black peppercorns
generous 6mm/¼ inch piece of cinnamon, broken in half
1 dried red chilli
300ml/10fl oz red wine vinegar
900g/2lb elderberries
1 onion, chopped
675g/1lb sugar
2 teaspoons sea salt

Place the cloves, allspice berries, peppercorns, cinnamon and chilli on a square of muslin and tie up with string to make a small bag. Add the muslin bag to a pan with the vinegar, cover the pan and bring the vinegar to the boil. Remove from the heat and leave overnight, covered, in a cool place.

Add the elderberries, onion, sugar and salt to the vinegar and simmer for about 10-15 minutes until the elderberries are tender. Remove the muslin bag from the pan and

*E*LDERBERRIES

Pheasant and Elderberry Casserole

The first time I made this recipe I prepared it by the method given below, the second time I put everything in a heavy non-metallic casserole, left it to marinate overnight then put it straight in the oven. Although the first result was better, the second casserole was quite acceptable. The cooking time in the oven will depend on the age of the bird.

SERVES 2

1 pheasant, jointed
small handful of herbs such as parsley, thyme, rosemary, chives
salt and freshly ground black pepper
350ml/12fl oz medium bodied red wine
1 tablespoon oil
115g/4oz thick cut bacon, chopped
1 onion, chopped
2 carrots, chopped
2 tablespoons Elderberry Sauce (see page 130)

Put the pheasant, herbs and seasonings in a non-metallic bowl, pour over the wine, cover and place in the refrigerator for about 8 hours, turning the bird over occasionally.

Preheat the oven to 150°C/300°F/gas mark 2. Remove the pheasant from the wine and dry thoroughly. Reserve the wine.

Heat the oil in a heavy flameproof casserole, add the bacon and fry until it is beginning to brown and the fat has been rendered. Add the onion and carrots and cook until lightly browned. Remove with a slotted spoon. Add the pieces of pheasant and brown lightly. Remove. Stir the wine, with the herbs, into the casserole and bring to the boil. Add the Elderberry Sauce. Return the pheasant then the vegetables and bacon to the casserole. Cover and cook in the oven until the pheasant is tender. If the sauce is not concentrated enough, remove the pheasant and keep warm then boil the sauce until sufficiently reduced.

sieve the sauce through a non-metallic sieve into a bowl. Return the sauce to the pan and cook over a moderate heat, stirring as necessary, until thickened. Pour into warm, clean, dry bottles and cover with vinegar-proof lids. Process in a waterbath for 30 minutes (see page 13).

Above: this Pheasant and Elderberry Casserole makes use of aromatic Elderberry Sauce to produce a richly flavoured dish which is simple to prepare.

Rosehip Syrup

According to country tradition, if rosehips are to be used in cooking, they should be picked after the first frost has hit them.

Rosehip syrup is very rich in Vitamin C, which is heat soluble, so the syrup is not made by the same method as other syrups but in a way that preserves the vitamin. Once opened, the syrup will not keep for more than a week or two so it is best to fill only small bottles.

MAKES ABOUT 570ML/1 PINT

900g/2lb ripe rosehips
450g/1lb warmed sugar (see page 7)

Bring 1.8 litres/3 pints water to the boil. Meanwhile, pass the rosehips through the coarse blade of a mincer, then immediately add to the water. Return to the boil and remove from the heat, then leave to infuse for 15 minutes.

Tip the contents of the pan into a scalded jelly bag suspended over a bowl and leave for 8-12 hours until most of the juice has strained through.

Return the rosehips in the jelly bag to the saucepan, add 850ml/1½ pints water and bring to the boil. Remove from the heat and leave for 10 minutes, then tip the contents of the pan back into the jelly bag and leave to strain again into the bowl for 4-6 hours.

Pour the juice into the rinsed pan and simmer until reduced to about 850ml/ 1½ pints.

Over a low heat, stir in the warmed sugar until it has dissolved. Raise the heat and boil for 5 minutes. Pour the syrup into hot bottles, cover and seal lightly. Process in a boiling waterbath for 5 minutes (see page 13). Remove the bottles from the waterbath and tighten the lids immediately. This will keep for up to 1 year.

About 2 teaspoons of the syrup a day is a pleasant, natural and cheap way of boosting the vitamin C content of the diet. This syrup is also good poured over sponge cake, stirred into fruit salads and poured over poached fruits.

Crystallized Rose Petals

Home-prepared crystallized rose petals look much better than bought ones. Egg white is sometimes used in place of gum arabic, but I find that gum arabic, which is available from chemists and specialist cake-decoration shops, is easier to apply to delicate petals and preserves them better and for longer. Other edible flower petals or small leaves, such as mint leaves, can be treated in the same way to use for decorating desserts, cakes and sweets.

6 large, fragrant roses
1 teaspoon gum arabic
about 3 teaspoons rose water
caster sugar

Separate the rose petals before carefully removing all of the white heels or bases. Dissolve the gum arabic in the rose water.

Coating rose petals with gum arabic solution: use a small brush to paint solution on to the petals, being careful to cover them completely.

Using an artist's or a make-up brush, gently brush the gum arabic solution over 3 or 4 petals at a time to cover completely. Dust with an even coating of sugar, making sure there are no patches left bare.

Leave on a foil-lined tray in a warm, dry, airy place, turning carefully, until quite dry. Store on tissue paper or paper towels inside an air-tight container. These will keep fresh for at least 1 year.

Rose Petal Jam

In the story of the Arabian Nights, the Caliph of Baghdad had seven palaces, the seventh and most sumptuous being the Palace of Eternal and Unsatiating Delights. At the feasts held there, one of the dishes that was served was a rose petal jam, the honeyed sweetness of which was supposed to have a secret power that held captive anyone who ate it. This jam may or may not be the same as that served at the palace, but it is certainly captivating. It is more like a thick syrup than a jam; if you would prefer a firmer set, use sugar with pectin, then boil for just 4 minutes.

MAKES ABOUT 450G/1LB

225g/8oz dark red, very fragrant roses
450g/1lb sugar
juice of 2 lemons
rose water to taste (optional)

Separate the rose petals, cut off the white heels, or bases, and chop the petals into small, but not too fine, pieces. Put the chopped petals in a bowl and stir in half the sugar. Cover and leave for about 24 hours.

In a pan, gently heat the remaining sugar in 1.1 litres/2 pints water and the lemon juice, stirring, until the sugar has dissolved. Add the rose petal mixture, raise the heat slightly and simmer gently for 20 minutes, stirring occasionally.

R OSES

Boil the petal mixture for 5 minutes until it is thickened, but has not reached setting point. Add rose water if the rose flavour is not strong enough. Ladle into warm, clean, dry jars. Cover and seal (see pages 12-13). Leave overnight to cool and set slightly. Store in a cool, dark, dry place.

Rose Petal Sorbet

Even in winter, it's easy to conjure up images of an old-fashioned country cottage garden on a midsummer's afternoon with this delicate sorbet, decorated with crystallized rose petals.

SERVES 4

225g/8oz sugar
about 3 tablespoons Rose Petal Jam
 (see page 132)
edible liquid red food colouring (optional)
Crystallized Rose Petals (see page 132),
 for decoration

Place the sugar together with 850ml/ 1½ pints water in a pan and heat gently, stirring, until all the sugar has dissolved. Stir in the Rose Petal Jam, raise the heat and boil until the mixture is syrupy (similar to the thickness of the syrup in canned fruits). Taste for rose flavour, remembering that freezing will mute it, and add more jam if necessary.

Pour the mixture into a shallow freezerproof container, leave to cool, then cover and chill in the fridge. Transfer to the freezer until just beginning to freeze. Remove from the freezer and tip into a chilled bowl. Whisk with a cold whisk to break up the ice crystals. Whisk in a little food colouring if the colour seems too pale. Return to the freezer and repeat once more, sealing the container tightly before final freezing. Serve decorated with a few of the Crystallized Rose Petals.

This unusual, delicate Rose Petal Sorbet is delightful, whether served on its own or accompanied by langues de chat, after a light summer meal. Serve in attractive glass bowls.

Above: this fragrant, subtly pink Rose Petal Sorbet makes a light, elegant and very special ending to a meal. It can also be served between courses as a refreshing palate cleanser.

*S*AFFRON, *G*INGER, *C*LOVES, *A*NGELICA

Saffron Garlic

This exotic preserve is very easy to make and provides a welcome alternative to ordinary pickles.

MAKES ABOUT 700ML/1¼ PINTS

4-5 garlic bulbs, separated into cloves
and peeled
3 tablespoons sugar
large pinch of saffron threads, crushed
1½ teaspoons black peppercorns
1 teaspoon sea salt

Bring 300ml/10fl oz water to the boil, then add the garlic and boil for 2 minutes.

Remove the pan from the heat. Scoop out the garlic with a slotted spoon. When they are cool enough to handle, peel and pack into a clean, dry, heatproof jar.

Add the sugar to the cooking water and heat gently, stirring, until the sugar has dissolved. Add the saffron, peppercorns and salt and bring quickly to the boil.

Pour over the garlic, cover and seal (see pages 12-13). Leave for at least 3 months before eating.

Rhubarb and Ginger Conserve

In Britain, ginger with rhubarb is considered a classic combination. I have used fresh ginger to give a background flavour and pieces of stem ginger to give a mellower, sweeter ginger taste to bite on. Be sure to choose a large piece of plump, firm fresh ginger with a sheen on the skin.

MAKES ABOUT 1.8KG/4LB

900g/2lb rhubarb, cut into small pieces
900g/2lb sugar
25g/1oz piece of fresh ginger, unpeeled
90g/3¼oz stem ginger, drained and chopped

Layer the rhubarb and sugar in a bowl, cover and leave in a cool place overnight.

Bruise the fresh ginger with the flat of a large knife on a chopping board then wrap it up in a muslin bag and put the bag in pan.

Tip the contents of the bowl into the pan. Heat gently, stirring until the sugar has dissolved. Raise the heat and boil hard for 15 minutes, stirring as necessary, until slightly thickened.

Add the stem ginger and boil for a further 5 minutes. Discard the muslin bag and remove any scum from the conserve with a slotted spoon. Leave the conserve to stand for 10-15 minutes. Ladle the conserve into warm, clean, dry jars. Cover and seal (see pages 12-13). Store in a cool, dark, dry place for at least 1 week before eating.

Quick and Easy Rhubarb Pickle

The rhubarb in this pickle is not heated to cook it but instead simply steeped in vinegar, which has the same effect as cooking. What could be easier? Moreover, the rhubarb keeps its shape and does not become soggy.

MAKES ABOUT 1.5KG/3¼LB

1.1kg/2½lb rhubarb, sliced
2 tablespoons sugar
2 tablespoons sea salt
575ml/1 pint cider vinegar
25g/1oz fresh ginger, thinly sliced
25g/1oz cloves
1 dried red chilli, broken up

Pack the rhubarb into a heatproof jar.

In a pan, gently heat the sugar and salt in the vinegar, stirring until the salt and sugar have dissolved. Add the spices and boil for 2 minutes.

Pour the hot vinegar over the rhubarb and leave to cool, then cover with a vinegar-proof lid and seal (see pages 12-13). Store in a cool, dark, dry place for at least 1 month before eating.

Candied Angelica

Home-made candied angelica is well worth the time and trouble it takes to prepare as it is so much better than the commercially prepared product. Angelica is easy to grow – I used to have a self-seeded one in a sunny patch of not-very-good, but well-drained soil in my old London garden. Each year it grew to a great height despite never being fed or watered, even in very dry spells. Pick the stems for candying in April or May and immediately drop them into the brine solution to preserve the colour; the leaves can be used to flavour cooked fresh fruit and have a sweetening effect on tart fruits, such as rhubarb (see Angelica and Rhubarb Jam, page 135). See pages 20-21 for step-by-step instructions on candying fruit.

8g/¼oz salt
a few handfuls of angelica stems
sugar

In a large bowl, stir the salt into 2.3 litres/4 pints water to dissolve, then add the angelica and leave for 10 minutes.

Drain the angelica and rinse under cold running water. Put in a pan with some cold water, bring to the boil, the boil for 5 minutes until quite tender. Drain, reserving the water, and transfer the angelica to a wire basket that will fit inside the pan. Once the angelica is cool, scrape the outer skin from each stem.

Put 175g/6oz sugar in the pan with 300ml/10fl oz of the reserved cooking water and heat gently, stirring until it has dissolved. Raise the heat and bring to the boil. Lower the angelica into the pan, cover

*A*NGELICA

and leave for 1 day in a cool place.

Lift the wire basket with the angelica out of the pan and measure the syrup – for every 300ml/10fl oz add 50g/2oz sugar – Return the syrup to the pan and heat it gently, stirring to dissolve the sugar. Raise the heat and bring to the boil. Remove from the heat and lower the angelica into the pan, cover and leave for a further day. Repeat this process another 5 times until the syrup is the consistency of thin honey, then boil

the angelica in the syrup for 2-3 minutes after the last 50g/2oz sugar has been dissolved. Cover and leave for 2 days.

Lift the angelica from the syrup (the syrup can be used to sweeten fruit dishes), place it on a wire rack covered with foil and leave to dry in a warm, dry place (or the oven set to its lowest setting with the door propped open with the handle of a wooden spoon). Store in an airtight container between layers of waxed paper.

Angelica and Rhubarb Jam

Fresh angelica not only produces a delightfully fragrant jam but it has a sweetening effect on the rhubarb.

MAKES ABOUT 1.4KG/3LB

900g/2lb rhubarb, sliced
900g/2lb sugar
5 angelica leaves, finely shredded
juice of 1 lemon

Stir the rhubarb and sugar together in a non-metallic bowl, then cover and leave to stand in a cool place for 8 hours.

Transfer the fruit and sugar to a saucepan, add the angelica and lemon juice and heat gently, stirring until the sugar has dissolved. Increase the heat and bring to the boil and continue to boil for 10-15 minutes, stirring as necessary, until setting point is reached.

Remove the jam from the heat and skim any scum from the surface with a slotted spoon. Ladle the jam into warm, clean, dry jars. Cover and seal (see pages 12-13). Store in a cool, dark, dry place for at least 1 month before eating.

Variation: *Rhubarb and Rose Petal Jam*
Use a good handful of fragrant dark red rose petals instead of the angelica and follow the recipe above. Makes about 1.4kg/3lb.

Use to fill a Victoria sandwich; in crisp tartlets topped with lightly whipped whipping cream; for an upside-down steamed sponge pudding or serve with coeurs à la crème.

Left: when preparing the rhubarb for Angelica and Rhubarb Jam, peel away any tough strings from the stalks before using; never eat the rhubarb leaves as they are poisonous.

Goats' Cheese in Oil

Leaving this to mature for 2-3 weeks before you open the jar ensures that all the oil takes on the full flavour of the cheese, and vice versa. To make this traditional French recipe, look for small and firm, but not dry, goats' cheeses that weigh roughly 60-75g/2½-3oz each.

MAKES 6

6 crottins de Chavignol, or other goats' cheese
2 bay leaves
3 sprigs of fresh thyme
1 sprig of fresh rosemary
1 garlic clove (optional)
6 black peppercorns
olive oil

Pack the cheeses, herbs, garlic, if using, and peppercorns into a clean, dry, wide-necked jar. Pour in oil to cover, close and seal the jar. Leave in a cool, dark, dry place for at least 1-2 weeks before using; use within 6-8 weeks.

Variation: *Feta Cheese in Oil*
Drain 175g/6oz feta cheese, dry well with paper towels and cut into cubes. Pack into clean, dry jars with several sprigs of mixed herbs, 1 dried red chilli, 2 lightly crushed garlic cloves and 12 black peppercorns. Pour over olive oil to cover. Cover and seal the jar and leave in a cool, dark, dry place for at least 1 week before using. Use within 6-8 weeks. Fills about one 500g/18oz jar.

Serve the cheese with crusty bread; add plain or toasted to salads; grill on toast; slice on to pizzas before baking; dice and toss with pasta. Any remaining oil left over after the goats' cheeses have been eaten can be used for salad dressings, trickled over firm, crusty bread or used for brushing grilled meats, chicken or fish or for sautéeing vegetables.

Flavoured Oils

Flavoured oils are very quick to make and wonderful to use for quickly adding interest and a personal touch to dishes.

Almost any aromatic flavouring can be used to add taste to oils, from rose petals, through fragrant herbs to aromatic spices and fiery chillies, to fruit zests. The choice of oil really depends on how the oil is to be used, on personal taste, and budget. For example, I like to flavour olive oils with herbs, choosing a virgin oil that I will use for salad dressings, and a non-virgin olive oil for cooking. Mild oils, such as corn and safflower, are more suitable for infusing with stronger flavourings.

Flavoured oils can be used for salad dressings, marinating, frying, brushing over foods to be grilled or baked and tossing with cooked vegetables.

Indian Spiced Oil

MAKES ABOUT 570ML/1 PINT

2 tablespoons coriander seeds
1 tablespoon fenugreek seeds
1 tablespoon cumin seeds
6 cardamom pods
2 dried red chillies
570ml/1 pint groundnut oil

Gently heat the spices and chillies in a dry heavy-based frying pan for about 5 minutes until fragrant, moving them gently around the pan to prevent them from catching.

Lightly crush the spices and chillies, then put them into a jar or bottle. Pour in the oil, seal tightly and shake to mix, then leave for about 1 week, shaking the jar or bottle occasionally, before using. The oil can now be strained and re-bottled, if liked. Store in a cool, dark, dry place for up to 6 months.

Herb Oil

Use either one type of herb or a mixture – if you want to use a mixture, add a couple of bay leaves to enhance the flavour.

MAKES ABOUT 1.1 LITRES/2 PINTS

small bunch of fresh herb sprigs, such as
rosemary, basil, tarragon, thyme
2 garlic cloves (optional)
6 black peppercorns
about 1.1 litres/2 pints olive oil

Put all the ingredients in a clean, dry jar or bottle, cover tightly and shake well to mix. Leave in a cool, dark place for 2 weeks, shaking the jar or bottle daily. Discard the garlic, if used. Re-cover and leave for a further 2 weeks.

Strain the oil and pour into a fresh clean, dry bottle. Add an appropriate herb sprig for decoration, if liked. Cover and store in a cool, dark, dry place. Use within 6 months.

Chilli Oil

Modify or increase the heat in this oil by adjusting the number of chillies or adding the chilli seeds. Chillies vary in their hotness, so taste the oil occasionally to see when it is hot enough.

If you want to use the oil immediately, slice the chillies, warm gently in the oil and then leave to infuse for 10 minutes or so.

MAKES ABOUT 570ML/1 PINT

about 8 fresh or dried red chillies, split
570ml/1 pint sunflower oil

Pack the chillies into a clean, dry bottle or jar, pour in the oil, cover and leave for about 2 weeks. Taste periodically and strain the oil when it is hot enough into another clean, dry bottle or jar. Store in a cool, dark, dry place and use within 6 months.

*F*LAVOURED OILS

Thai Oil

MAKES ABOUT 700ML/1¼ PINTS

4 pieces of lemon grass
4 sprigs of fresh coriander
2 dried red chillies, split
1 garlic clove
700ml/1¼ pints sunflower oil

Lightly bruise the lemon grass with the flat of a large knife on a chopping board. Lightly crush the coriander between your hands, then put into a jar or bottle with the lemon grass, chillies and garlic. Pour in the oil, cover tightly and shake well, then leave for 2 weeks. Discard the garlic (use a long skewer to spear it). Re-cover and seal. The oil is now ready for using. Store in a cool dark, dry place and use within 6 months.

Spiced Orange Oil

MAKES ABOUT 700ML/1¼ PINTS

3 wide strips orange zest
1 tablespoon coriander seeds
700ml/1¼ pints olive oil

Preheat the oven to its lowest setting. Put the orange zest on a baking sheet and put in the oven for about 1¼ hours to dry out; add the coriander seeds to the baking sheet for the last 30 minutes or so until fragrant.

Lightly crush the coriander seeds using a mortar and pestle or a small blender and put into a jar or bottle with the zest, cut if necessary to fit into the neck of the jar or bottle. Pour in the oil, seal tightly and shake to mix, then leave for about 2 weeks, taking care to shake the jar or bottle occasionally. Store in a cool, dark, dry place and use within 6 months.

Left (from left to right): Herb Oil, Thai Oil, Spiced Orange Oil and Indian Spiced Oil.

Herb Jellies

I like to make a range of herb jellies so I always have the appropriate one for serving with different types of meat – sage for pork, mint or rosemary for lamb, tarragon or thyme for chicken, parsley for ham. You can make the jellies as strongly flavoured as you like by adjusting the amount of chopped herbs you add.

1.1kg/2½lb cooking apples, preferably Bramleys
a few large sprigs of the chosen herb or a mixture of herbs
570ml/1 pint white wine vinegar
sugar
medium-sized bunch of herbs, finely chopped to make 3-4 tablespoons

Chop the apples without peeling or coring them. Put the apples into a pan with the herb sprigs and 570ml/1 pint water. Bring to the boil, then simmer gently for about 1 hour, stirring occasionally. Add the vinegar to the pan, bring to the boil and boil for 5 minutes.

Tip the contents of the pan into a scalded jelly bag suspended over a non-metallic bowl and leave to strain, undisturbed, in a cool place for 8-12 hours.

Measure the juice and put it into a pan with 450g/1lb sugar for every 570ml/1 pint juice. Heat the juice gently, stirring, until the sugar has dissolved, then raise the heat and boil hard for 10-15 minutes until setting point is reached (see page 17).

Remove the pan from the heat and skim the scum from the surface with a slotted spoon. Leave the jelly to stand for 10-15 minutes, then stir in the chopped herbs. Ladle into warm, clean, dry jars. Cover and seal (see pages 12-13). Leave overnight to cool and set slightly. Store in a cool, dark, dry place.

Flavoured Vinegars

Vinegars infused with aromatic flavourings are as easy to make as flavoured oils (see pages 136-7), but they can be kept for at least 1 year. Use them to give individuality to salad dressings and for making mayonnaise. Be sure that flowers and herbs are completely dry before using.

Citrus Vinegar

MAKES ABOUT 1 LITRE/1¾ PINTS

1 litre/1¾ pints white wine vinegar
2 lemons
½ orange
2 limes
pinch of paprika
pepper
sea salt

Pour the vinegar into a pan. Thinly slice 1 lemon and add to the pan. Grate the zest from the other lemon, the ½ orange and the limes into the pan. Squeeze the juice from 1 lime into the pan. Add the paprika, pepper and salt and bring to the boil. Leave to cool.

Pour into clean, dry jars, distributing the lemon slices evenly. Cover with vinegar-proof lids and leave in a sunny or warm place for 2 weeks, shaking the jars occasionally. Strain through a non-metallic sieve lined with muslin, then pour into clean, dry bottles.

Chilli Vinegar

MAKES 1 LITRE/1¾ PINTS

350g/12oz mixed red and green chillies
1 litre/1¾ pints white wine vinegar
2-3 garlic cloves

Put the chillies and the vinegar in a pan and boil for 1 minute.

Put the garlic in clean, dry bottles and pour in the vinegar. Cover and seal with vinegar-proof lids. Store the vinegar for 2-4 weeks before using, shaking the bottle occasionally. Store in a cool, dark, dry place.

Elderflower Vinegar

MAKES ABOUT 1 LITRE/1¾ PINTS

generous bunch of elderflower heads (umbels)
1 litre/1¾ pints white wine vinegar, to cover

Pack the elderflowers into a clean, dry bottle or jar. Pour in the vinegar to cover, then cover with a vinegar-proof lid and seal. Leave in a cool, dark, dry place for at least 1 month.

Strain through a non-metallic sieve lined with muslin, then pour into a clean, dry bottle. Cover and seal. Store in a cool, dark, dry place.

Old-fashioned Rose Petal Vinegar

MAKES ABOUT 1 LITRE/1¾ PINTS

75g/3oz highly scented rose petals
1 litre/1¾ pints white wine vinegar

Pack the rose petals into a large clean, dry jar and pour in the vinegar to cover. Close the jar with a vinegar-proof lid and leave to infuse for about 10 days, shaking the jar occasionally.

Strain the vinegar through a non-metallic sieve lined with muslin, then pour it into clean, dry bottles. Cover the bottles with vinegar-proof lids. The vinegar can now be used. Store in a cool, dark, dry place.

FLAVOURED VINEGARS

Spiced Vinegar

The primary use for this vinegar is in pickling, but it can also be used to make salad dressings and mayonnaise.

MAKES ABOUT 1.1 LITRES/2 PINTS

1 tablespoon allspice berries
1 tablespoon cloves
2 cinnamon sticks
1 tablespoon black peppercorns
2 blades of mace
2 bay leaves, torn
4 dried red chillies
1.1 litres/2 pints red or white wine vinegar

Put all the spices, the bay leaves, the chillies and the vinegar in a pan and bring to the boil. Pour into clean, dry bottles, distributing the flavourings evenly. Cover with vinegar-proof lids and seal (see pages 12-13). The vinegar can be used after 1 day, but it is better to leave it for 1-2 weeks before using. Store in a cool, dark, dry place.

If the vinegar is kept for some time, check the flavour and if it is becoming too strong, strain out the flavourings.

Below (from left to right): Chilli, Old-fashioned Rose Petal, Citrus and Spiced Vinegars.

General Index

Page numbers in *italics* refer to the illustrations

Recipes in *italics* refer to usage recipes

Index by Type of Preserve

Page numbers in *italic* refer to the illustrations

Useful addresses

Adnams Cellar and Kitchen Store
Victoria Street
Southwold
Suffolk 1P18 6JW
Tel: 01502 727 220 (mail order)

Le Chef
10 Nile Street
Brighton
Sussex BN1 1HW
Tel: 01273 771219

Elizabeth David Cookshop
3A North Row
London WC2E 8RU
Tel: 0171 836 9167 (mail order)

Elizabeth David Cookshop
Nason's of Canterbury Ltd
46-7 High Street
Canterbury
Kent CT1 2SB
Tel: 0122 745 6755 (mail order)

Divertimenti Retail Ltd
45-7 Wigmore Street
London W1H 9LE
Tel: 0171 935 0689

Lakeland Plastics
Alexandra Buildings
Windermere
Cumbria LA23 1BQ
Tel: 015394 88100 (mail order)

John Lewis (for details of stores
nationwide contact: 0171 629
7711)

David Mellor Design Ltd
4 Sloane Square
London SW1W 8EE
Tel: 0171 730 4259 (mail order)

Harvey Nichols & Co. Ltd
109-125 Knightsbridge
London SW1X 7RJ
Tel: 0171 235 5000

Pages Catering Equipment
121 Shaftesbury Avenue
London WC2H 8AD
Tel: 0171 379 6334 (mail order)

Alan Silverwood Ltd
Ledsam House,
Birmingham B16 8DN
Tel: 0121 454 3571 (for stockists)

A. B. E Staines Catering Equipment
15-19 Brewer Street
London W1R 3FL
Tel: 01734 304 848 (mail order)

Wild Food Tamed
Tel: 01672 870 639 or 0171 735
4475 (supplier of wild fruits, nuts
and herbs; pickles and pastes)

AUSTRALIA

David Jones Department Stores
in Sydney, Melbourne, Adelaide and
Brisbane
Tel: (2) 266 5544 (Sydney)

Mitre 10 Home Hardware Stores
in Sydney, Melbourne, Adelaide and
Brisbane
Tel: (2) 725 3222 (Sydney)

Author's Acknowledgments

During the research and writing of this
book I came across many people who
had one or two treasured preserve
recipes. Without exception they were
willing to pass these on, and I thank every
one very much. I always asked if the
recipes came from a published source and
have credited these wherever possible.
The recipes for Ratatouille Chutney (see
page 36) and Honey Spiced Pickled
Oranges (see page 66) originated from
ones created by Jackie Burrows in *Home
Preserves*, first published in 1979 by
Sundial Books Limited as part of the
St Michael Cookery Library.

Publisher's Acknowledgments

The publisher would like to thank the
following: Kate Bell, Alison Bolus, Jo
Brewer, Janet Brinkworth, Jackie Burrows,
Fiona Kirkpatrick, Louisa Maskill of Wild
Food Tamed (for supplying green walnuts
for the photograph on page 127), Jackie
Matthews and Kate Worsley. The publisher
also thanks: Jane Chapman, Alison Fenton,
Helen Green and Tony Seddon.